Christopher S. Blomgren

S.O.S.

CHRISTOPHER BLOMGREN

SURVIVAL and BEYOND FOR THE
CHRISTIAN ADVENTURER

WINTERS
PUBLISHING GROUP

Published by Winters Publishing
2448 E. 81st St.
Suite #4802
Tulsa, OK 74137

Book Design Copyright 2014 by Winters Publishing. All rights reserved.
Cover design by Jan Sunday Quilaquil
Interior design by Caypeeline Casas

Published in the United States of America

ISBN: 978-1-62994-497-5
Religion / Christian Life
14.01.31

ACKNOWLEDGEMENTS

The mastery of survival begins with a positive mindset, is honed through the practicing of skills, and is strengthened by the acquisition of equipment. In writing this book, my mindset was constantly kept positive by the support of my loving wife, Mary; she is my greatest source of earthly joy. My dear friend, Nancy Raca, as she has since kindergarten, also served as a pillar of support and encouragement when obstacles sought to dissuade me.

The practice of skills (i.e. the joyous pursuits of semi-reckless behavior) found me in constant fellowship with David Holdridge. There is no man I would rather assault the gates of hell with than he. Yarden Weidenfeld is another companion not unfamiliar with adventure. He bears the distinction of almost suffering decapitation on account of our recreational antics (although, if you're honest with yourself, Yarden, the second time wasn't my fault!) Shalom, brother.

The "acquisition of equipment" necessary for the production of this book comes through the good people of Winters Publications. Thank you for your hard work, attention to detail, and insight.

As always, any positive outcomes that may result from my work I dedicate with gratitude to the ultimate expert on survival and the preserver of life: my lord and savior, Christ Jesus.

CONTENTS

PREFACE

I live on a small piece of farm property in upstate New York. Accompanying me on this six-acre plot of paradise are my wife and kids, four chickens, three horses, two guinea pigs, a dog, cat…and a single apple tree.

One apple tree. I'm not sure how it got there or how old it is, perhaps some remnant of what might have been an orchard back in the seventies. It's gnarled and twisted, standing all alone, and in a good season it yields perhaps four edible apples.

My neighbor is a retired arborist, a great resource to have if, like me, you know very little about trees. One day he and I were walking the property, and I showed him the apple tree, lamented the fact that it was so unproductive, and asked if there were any way I might improve its output. He studied it briefly, examining its un-manicured branches and ragged bark. Then he looked up and said, "You need to prune it. Prune it right down next to nothing. If you want a tree to bear fruit, it must be convinced that its very life is in danger, that it is in jeopardy of ever seeing another season."

And so, not for the first time in creation, an eloquent and simple truth was presented to man through the wood of a tree: if you desire to produce fruit, you must prune everything of secondary importance back and focus on what truly matters. No one has been guaranteed another season, indeed even another day. You must be convinced that your very life is in jeopardy; you are in a survival situation.

This is a survival manual. It is written with the intent that that those who are lost might find their way, that those who are weary might find solace, and that those in dire circumstances might find encouragement. In short, its purpose is to save lives. However, if you are looking for help building animal snares, finding your way using the stars or learning the finer points of constructing a snow cave, then you have the wrong book. Many such publications already exist, written by those with far greater experience and qualification. And in truth, the focus of this book is not the preservation of flesh and blood.

This is a training manual. Within these pages lie reflective memoirs, challenging questions, and practical advice, all utilizing the metaphor of survival. It speaks of hopeful people in hopeless situations, of harrowing escapes and near misses. There is danger and suffering, despair and redemption; in short, everything that you would expect from a survival story. Again, its purpose is to save lives.

This is a Christian devotional. I take seriously the sacrifice of my personal rescuer, Jesus Christ, the mission of His Church, and the vocation of teaching given to me through the grace of the Holy Spirit (Romans 12:6-7). I am not a minister or preacher, nor do I hold a degree in theology. I have no dramatic story of personal conversion or indeed, any truly unique insight of any kind (Ecclesiastes 1:9-10). I'm just a guy with a wife and two wonderful daughters. I work with at-risk youth, some of whom could tell survival stories that rival any in this book, and in my spare time I read history books and vacuum dog hair off the living room carpet.

I've taken a few courses from some top-notch instructors, played around in the military and helped some people out of some tight spots, and every once in a while, I get to go off with a canoe and flintlock musket and lose myself in the backwoods. However, my only real qualification is one that I share with many of you: I'm a curious guy who has made a lot of mistakes, none of which have killed me, and most of which I've learned from.

If this work creates in you a stronger hunger for God and dependence on Christ, I am humbled. If you find error in this work and correct me gently, I am grateful. And in all matters that strengthen our companionship and walk in the Lord, I offer Him praise.

—Christopher S. Blomgren
Palmyra, New York
Spring, 2013

PART I:

SURVIVAL PRINCIPLES AND PARABLES

Every course of instruction begins with a foundation. Whether it's learning jiu-jitsu, horsemanship, or small engine repair, it is crucial to have an understanding of basic principles. Without this understanding, you may be performing all the correct steps and even seeing desirable results, but your efforts will be haphazard and any success that does occur will be more through chance than by design. It reminds me of the words of St. Paul: "...do not run like one who runs aimlessly or box like one beating the air" (1Cornthians: 9-26).

Part I takes a look at six survival principles. They are written within the context of physical survival, but as you study each section, remember to dig deeper into the parable presented and reflect upon its application to the spiritual.

I

ACKNOWLEDGE THE CRISIS

Crisis: A time when a difficult or important decision must be made.

Oxford English Dictionary

As a younger man I served as an infantry officer in the United States Army. My job description was simple: shoot, move and communicate in such a way as to inflict maximum damage on the enemy and accomplish the mission. In 1990 while on a desert night exercise, this translated into reconnoitering a brigade of enemy armored vehicles and reporting their movement to company headquarters. And so I left my platoon in a defensive perimeter and took my radio telephone operator (RTO) with me to recon a route through a *wadi*, the steep desert canyons that laced this area. It was a frustrating labyrinth for anyone wishing to follow a compass bearing, and sometimes it became necessary to climb the steep walls out of a wadi in order to stay on azimuth. To do so quietly, at night, with 80 pounds of equipment on my back proved daunting, to say the least.

This was the situation I faced about 0100 hours. The walls of the canyon were treacherous with loose shale and I knew it would be extremely difficult to ascend the walls with my rucksack and M-16 rifle and impossible for my RTO to climb beside me with the extra weight of the radio. So I directed him to remain below with all our gear while I scaled the walls to survey the area.

The climb was precarious. Despite the loose nature of the rock wall, desert cacti still managed to grow at sporadic intervals and were impossible for me to spot on the craggy cliff face. I tried not to wince as the insidious needles easily and unpredictably pierced my gloves. Sometimes the thick leather would prove adequate protection, not so the cotton knees of my desert-weight BDU trousers, and it was with no small relief that I reached the top.

With its crystal-clear sky, the desert becomes surprisingly cold at night, and I began to shiver as I adjusted my PVS-7 night vision device (NVDs). The ambient light of the stars fed into my goggles and cast everything in the eerie green light that is night vision. The sand was as soft and fine as baby powder, and I swept my bare hand back and forth in front of me. But as I did so, I saw something that caused me to freeze in mid-sweep: two or three inches from my hand a creature scuttled away silently into the night. Its translucent body made it near-invisible, but I could still discern the wide open claws and arachnid tail twitching nervously above. In the still of the desert night I could barely make out the sound of the sand granules as the scorpion continued on its quest for food. Somewhat shaken, I made my scan of the desolate landscape and began my descent.

Now every time I brushed against a cactus or even a sharp rock on the route down the cliff face, my imagination screamed, *Scorpion!* Consequently, I did not move perhaps as quietly as I should have, but I sure moved quickly. Upon reaching the bottom I glanced about for my RTO. He was gone. As a matter of fact, my rucksack and rifle were gone, too. This was not part of the contingency plan I left him prior to the climb. Not good. After a cursory search, it quickly became apparent that he had returned to the patrol base without me.

As I began to work my way through the wadi back to base my mind began to fill with furious thoughts toward my RTO. His sole military purpose was to always be within arm's length of me, ready to hand me the radio headset the moment I extended my hand. My pace quickened to a slow trot, as did my pulse, as I envisioned the rage I would unleash on Private First Class McIdiot. What kind of fool deserts his platoon leader and goes wandering around by himself? And why did he take all my gear with him? How could he even carry all my gear? What kind of idiot...I slowly looked around at the unfamiliar desert landscape, and as I did so, a thought struck me with the rapidity of a scorpion strike: *What kind of idiot platoon leader trots through the featureless desert cursing the stupidity of others even as he becomes hopelessly lost...*

Three hours later. Three weary hours of backtracking, wandering the maze of twisting canyons and feeling the tendrils of panic slowly overcome rational thought. I reached for my one-quart canteen and took a deep draught of lukewarm water. And in doing so, I did what I should have done three hours earlier: I paused. I paused and knelt beside a lone clump of desert brush to get my act together, wincing as yet another wicked thorn pierced into my shredded knee. But even before the sound of a whispered curse could leave my sun burnt lips, I heard a noise that caught my breath short. From somewhere in the night came the rumble of diesel engines.

Armored vehicles. Somewhere in the dark, tanks and armored personnel carriers beginning to surge forward like prehistoric metal beasts. I didn't know how far away they were, it can be very difficult to gauge the distance of sounds in the still desert air, but this much I did know: there were no friendly armored vehicles in our area of operations. Another thing I knew: infantrymen who fall asleep in tank country don't always wake up. The driver of a sixty-ton armored vehicle would notice the crushing of a sleeping body less than I would notice the crushing of a scorpion beneath my jungle boot.

At this point I heard another, even more insidious rumbling. It was a voice, a whisper really. I don't know how long it had been speaking, unheeded, inside my head, but now it seemed to grasp me tightly around my Kevlar helmet chin strap and rivet my attention: *You're lost and alone. Inadequately equipped, unarmed and* *exhausted. The enemy is unseen and prowling the night. You're afraid…*Acknowledge the crisis.

Reflection

At the beginning of most survival scenarios there is a single moment, sometimes sharply defined, other times developing gradually—when we experience a dramatic pause. Perhaps it is after the echo of explosions or gunshots has stilled. It could be when cries of anger and pain have been reduced to whimpers of fear. The blank acknowledgment of a stomach or a gas gauge that reads empty. The final signing of a divorce paper. Or a doctor slowly shaking his head: "I'm so sorry…" It is a moment of epiphany. It is the moment when we are asked to confirm what we have probably suspected for some time: This situation is beyond our ability to control.

What we do at this critical juncture will impact the rest of our life, and either consciously or subconsciously we know this. There is a life in the balance: our own. The next few moments, the next few decisions may determine if we are survivor or victim. And it doesn't matter whether the danger is physical, emotional or spiritual, because the first step to take is always the same. We have to say to ourselves: I'm in peril and need help.

An easy first step, right? You'd have to be a fool not to admit you're in trouble…Yet, if you're honest with yourself, there's a pretty good chance that there's been a time when you refused to acknowledge the crisis. Why? Why would we sabotage ourselves like this? The reasons are all too many:

Shock: "I'm so overwhelmed by pain/grief/emotion that I can't even comprehend the danger. My defense against this crisis is to encapsulate myself within a shell of disbelief. Numbness is the best defense against pain."

Pride: "This sort of thing couldn't possibly happen to me; I'm much too clever to find myself in a situation like this. And even if this is happening to me, I can handle it with my own resources."

Despair: "What's the point? This problem is so overwhelming that no matter what I do I'm doomed. Nobody could possibly help me, and frankly, I'm not even sure I'm worthy of being saved anyway."

Ignorance: "Danger? What danger? Why is that snake wiggling its butt with some kind of rattling sound? It's just a little lightning, and this tree is so dry and comfy. She would never leave me; why would she leave me?"

There are other reasons, I'm sure, but snaking its way in and amongst all of them is the demon of fear. Fear is the opposite of faith, whispering in your ear: You will fail, there is no hope. You will disappoint and you will suffer. No one will hear your cries, and you will surely die.

It is fear that paralyzes us from taking the first step. It is fear that prevents us from initiating the chain of decisions necessary to becoming a survivor: the woman who will not jump out of the burning building into the safety net below. The child who will not reach out from the swamped canoe to his father's hand on shore. The apostle who hesitates to take his eyes from the raging sea and reach out to his Savior…

You want to take the first step to becoming a survivor? The first leap to physical, emotional or spiritual rescue will likely be made in fear. Acknowledge it. Acknowledge the danger, the crisis you are already in, and step forward.

Discussion:

1. Man's first crisis began with an act of disobedience: the consumption of forbidden fruit (Genesis 3). When in your life has disobedience resulted in crisis? What was Adam's response to his crisis? What was yours?

2. It is often beneficial to share a crisis moment with a spouse or loved one. But are there certain times when you ought to acknowledge a crisis to God and God alone?

3. In Matthew 4:17, Jesus begins His public ministry with the declaration, "...Repent, for the kingdom of heaven is near." Does this command to repent tie into the concept of acknowledging crisis?

4. Reread the definition of crisis at the beginning of this chapter. Did Jesus experience times of crisis? If so, how did He acknowledge the crisis?

5. How do men acknowledge crisis different than women? Why? How does this affect relationships?

6. "A person strong in their faith is less likely to encounter crisis." Do you agree with this statement?

7. A crisis in the desert sparked my faith. In stripping me of my pride and control, I came to know God more intimately. Has there ever been a "desert crisis" in your life?
8. Does God deliberately put us into crisis situations? Explain.

Quotations for Reflection:

1. "Seeds of faith are always within us; sometimes it takes a crisis to nourish and encourage their growth." Susan Taylor
2. "There cannot be a crisis today; my schedule is already full." Henry Kissinger
3. "In crises the most daring course is often the safest." Kissinger
4. "The crisis of today is the joke of tomorrow." H.G. Wells
5. "Conflict builds character. Crisis defines it." Steven Thulon
6. "The hottest places in Hell are reserved for those who, in a period of moral crisis, maintain their neutrality." Dante

Scripture for Reflection:

1. Luke 23:38-42. Two different reactions to a crisis.

2. Psalm 69:13-18. Even a king must acknowledge crisis.
3. Nehemiah 2:17. Acknowledgement leads to action.

II

CHOOSE LIFE:
FROM VICTIM TO SURVIVOR

"Where a man can live, there also can he live well."

—Marcus Aurelius

Ever hear of a guy named Hugh Glass? Think early 1800's America. Rocky Mountains fur trapper kind of guy: buckskin shirt, beaver hat, black powder rifle... you get the picture. Hugh was a member of a fur trapping brigade trespassing through dangerous country. The Arikara Nation was not particularly pleased about interlopers crossing their lands, and to be discovered at this time would likely result in a bullet or arrow through your chest. There were a lot of ways to die in the wilderness of the West: Indian attack, blizzards, starvation, disease, swollen rivers...

And grizzly bear. An animal of such size and power, it was held in awe by Native Americans and trappers alike. Picture a carnivore that weighs in at 1,500 pounds.

Six inch claws connected to arms with the power to break a buffalo's neck with one swipe. Standing twelve feet tall, it fears no other creature on the continent, and why should it? In the land of the West, the grizzly is the supreme monarch.

It was such a creature that fell upon Hugh Glass. Probably a sow, defending her cubs, she began tearing into Hugh before he could bring his rifle into play. He fought for his life with fist and knife against the bear's fangs and claws. Hugh's companions came running at the sound of what must have been horrific screams. There is no terror quite like the fear of being torn apart by wild beasts. The Romans knew this when they wrapped condemned Christians in animal skins and unleashed ravenous dogs upon them. Perhaps Daniel knew this when he was flung into a den of starving lions. And Hugh surely knew this as he found the flesh being ripped from his body.

The fellow mountain men shot repeatedly into the head of the she-grizzly until convinced of her demise. Beneath her lay the lifeless body of Hugh Glass. The skin of his scalp had been torn almost completely from his skull. He was lacerated by those six inch daggers from head to ankle. His leg was snapped in half. His ribs lay exposed with little flesh left to cover them. The life was rapidly fading from his mangled remains, and all this in the heart of enemy territory. The party came to a difficult decision: Hugh Glass would have to be abandoned to die. So two men were left to dig his grave and minister to him, and the rest of the brigade continued on to the Yellowstone. The men dug a hasty grave and waited for Hugh to die. But Hugh would not die. Three days passed and he broke into a fierce fever as his wounds began to fester. But somewhere in his semi-conscious brain Hugh had chosen to survive.

Fearing Indian attack, the two men tending him came to a logical conclusion: Hugh was as good as dead; why should they die as well while waiting for the inevitable? So they covered him in a bear skin, leaves and soil. They took his rifle and all his gear, and they left him to die.

But Hugh chose to live. He stirred into consciousness and crawled over to a rotten log. Rolling onto the dead tree, he allowed maggots to consume his infection-ridden back. He set his own leg. Then he began, in a crawl, to work his way to the nearest settlement, Fort Kiowa. It was over two hundred miles away.

Hugh chose to live. He fed himself on berries and the flesh of raw rattlesnake. He was nearly trampled in a buffalo stampede, nearly discovered by the hostile Arikara, nearly died from fever, exposure, starvation and blood loss.

Hugh chose to live. His crawl became a staggering limp. He floated down the Cheyenne River on a fallen tree. He continued on the Missouri River. Months had passed when at last he reached the fort, his skeletal body a living witness to what a man can endure. At some point along his epic journey, he went from being Hugh Glass, victim of the wilderness, to Hugh Glass, survivor. Choose life: move from victim to survivor.

Reflection

Why is it that some people survive where others perish? How can some overcome the harshest of environments with the most limited of resources whereas others collapse in a heap of self-defeat? Think of the kid who grows up in an abusive household, struggling through poverty, neglect and deprivation; yet, he somehow grows up to be a caring and responsible citizen, a loving family man. Contrast this with the media idol, surrounded by wealth and adoration, with resources and opportunity beyond belief, only to burn out in a conflagration of drugs, affairs, self-loathing and despair.

It makes for an interesting discussion. How much of our mental toughness is innate from birth? How much does environment play upon our ability to overcome adversity? Why does pressure cause some to collapse like a soda can while causing others to harden into diamonds?

I don't have any easy answers, but this much I am convinced of: survival is a decision. Even if a person physically perishes, he ultimately remains a survivor so long as he dies with the mentality of a survivor. And what is that mindset? What is a survivor? A survivor is one who recognizes that we are living in a war zone, that hostile forces are arrayed against us, and that the fight is unavoidable. Christ Himself warns us that conflict and division are inevitable, that fire will come upon the earth and the very fabric of society will be utterly rent apart (Luke 12:49-53).

But in the midst of the maelstrom, a survivor endures. In the eye of the storm there is a peace, because it is not about winning the battle, it is about winning the war, and a survivor is able to look past this present danger and see what lies beyond. Survival is victory, and victory comes not from the avoidance of trial, but from the overcoming of it. Flesh may succumb to insurmountable odds, but for the one who has chosen life, and life in abundance, there is no final defeat.

There are many times in life when we have no choice. Nobody asks for illness, unemployment, natural disaster or broken relationships. But since the days of the Garden we have always been given the opportunity to choose a mindset, a way that leads to life or a way that leads to ultimate despair. The second step on our path of survival is to accept a simple invitation that has been laid before us all: Choose life: move from victim to survivor.

Discussion:

1. What is the difference between a victim and a survivor?
2. In nature, how does a predator select its victim?
3. Scripture speaks of the devil prowling about looking for someone to devour (1Peter2:8). How does the devil select his victims?
4. Your son is being victimized by the school bully. What steps would you take to train him how to move from victim to survivor mode?

5. What does it mean to "choose life"? What would this look like on a daily basis?
6. How do you respond to someone who declares that, because of tremendous suffering, life is not worth living?
7. Does surviving a crisis make you more resilient in dealing with future crises or does it merely wear you down?

Quotes for Reflection:

1. "I'm a survivor. At least that's what everyone tells me." Courtney Love
2. "Life stinks; but it sure beats the alternative." Anonymous
3. "Life is something that everyone should try at least once." Henry J. Tillman
4. "It is not necessary to change. Survival is not mandatory." W. Edwards Deming

Scripture for Reflection:

1. Deuteronomy 30:19. God, through Moses, offers us a choice.
2. 2Kings 18:32. There are other voices that will offer invitations to other paths, paths that are smooth and appealing, but ultimately lead to death
3. Revelation 3:15-16. A failure to choose is the course of cowards and victims.

III

SEND OUT A DISTRESS CALL

> May Day: An international distress call only to
> be used in a life-threatening situation. Derived
> from the French, M'aidez, meaning, "Come and
> help me."
>
> —John Wiseman

Apocryphal: derived from the French, Mon Dieu, meaning, "My God!"

Here is an interesting thing about the North Atlantic Ocean: because of the impurities found within the water (primarily salt), and because it takes a great deal of energy exchange to transfer water from one state of matter to another, often one finds liquid temperatures *below* thirty two degrees Fahrenheit. Like on April 14, 1912. On this moonless night the water temperature was four degrees below freezing.

Here is an interesting thing about the human body: our bodies are in such a state of equilibrium that, should our internal temperatures be changed by a mere seven degrees in either direction, we would almost certainly perish. For example, accidental immersion in frigid water of say, four degrees below freezing, would force us to gasp as we began shivering and producing goose bumps. This involuntary muscular activity would be woefully inadequate to raise our core temperature, and the body would exhibit symptoms very similar to alcoholic intoxication: mental confusion sometimes actually causes victims to strip off warm clothing and life jackets; cries for help grow inaudible as speech begins to slur; disorientation causes people to swim away from rescuers and safety; and in mere minutes lethargy leads to apathy becomes unconsciousness and ends in death.

Jack Phillips and Harold Bride were probably dimly aware of this as they went about their business. They were Marconi radio operators aboard the RMS *Titanic*. The Marconi radio was a state of the art wireless telegraph operating at 1,500 watts, and with this kind of power it was quite capable of transmitting and receiving over considerable distances, like the 58 miles to *The Carpathia*. Using Morse code, a series of audible dots and dashes, the standard distress call of the day was sent: CQD. CQ was essentially radiospeak for: every station listen to what follows. The D was the code letter for distress. Thus, CQD: all receivers listen: We are in imminent danger of death. Help us.

Several ships heard and responded, but none that responded were closer than *The Carpathia*, four hours distant. The radio operators and crew tried several other distress signals: rocket flares, a Morse code lamp. Someone suggested the relatively new international distress code: SOS. Officially established in 1908, many today assume that SOS actually stands for something, perhaps Save Our Ship, or Save Our Souls. In reality, it is not an abbreviation for anything. The series of 3 dots, dashes and dots (...—-...) does not even really represent the letters S, O and S, because it is incorrect to even briefly pause while transmitting this distress sequence as you would when transmitting individual letters. It was purposely designed this way for only one thing: to send a clear, unambiguous, unmistakable signal of distress. SOS: we are in imminent danger of death. Help us.

The sinking of the RMS *Titanic* is usually remembered as a human tragedy, and rightfully so. More than 1,500 human beings were lost that night. It is also thought of as a bitter reminder of the disastrous effects of human arrogance again, rightfully so. Thought unsinkable, it was not deemed necessary to have sufficient lifeboats on hand.

But there is another, oft-ignored element to this maritime drama, and that is this: a cry for help was raised and answered. Rescue efforts were made. Acts of heroism and self-sacrifice occurred. And for those who were rescued from the ocean's icy tomb, it didn't matter what CQD or SOS really stood for. All they knew was that they cried out for a rescuer to Save Our Souls, a cry that was heard, a cry that was answered. Send out a distress call.

Reflection

As a youth, it was always difficult for me to ask for help, and in that respect I think I was like most young boys. It didn't matter whether it was asking my sister for help on a math problem (made even worse by the fact that it was my younger sister), letting my mom show me the proper way to spoon out cookie dough onto a greased pan (mmm…cookie dough), or having my buddy give me tips on how to play the latest video game (I believe it was called, "Pong"). The point was if I asked for help, it was a clear demonstration of weakness. It declared to the whole world that my resources, my training, my natural abilities were inadequate, and who wants to do that?

Progressing to early manhood only intensifies the problem because now the delusion of self-reliance tends to solidify. After all, you've got your own source of income, your own set of wheels and your own little bachelor pad, complete with a cupboard filled with instant macaroni and cheese. And if you're living on a college campus, you've really got it made, because now you're surrounded by equally deluded peers who also feel like they're self-reliant, and they will be happy to celebrate this fact with you over a glass of brew and a trip next door to the all-female dormitory. Cry out for help? SOS? Are you kidding me? Life doesn't get much better than this!

Christians who have faithfully attended church, youth group, teen retreats and such all their lives often experience a falling away in their late teens. Why? Well, perhaps for the same reason that many turned away from the Church as the Dark Ages gave way to the Renaissance: the sense of dependence on God is replaced by the non-sense of independence through Man. We're young. The merchants, entertainers, and culture of this world are vying for our attention. We're strong, healthy, and eager to discard the security blanket of childhood and replace it with the cloak of adulthood. This means throwing off the smothering love of parents, the rigidity of morality, and the tired, outdated restraints of God. It is a time to question authority and experience life for ourselves. We're cruising on a course that seems true, on a vessel that boasts the best of what Man has to offer, on a sea that appears calm and tranquil. Why on earth would we need any lifeboats? Sound familiar? Do yourself a favor: take a look below the waterline.

Here is a difficult reality for many: God wants us to remain dependent on Him. There will never be a point that I can turn off the SOS signal and say, "Don't worry, God. I can take it from here." This is a difficult lesson to accept because our human experiences teach us otherwise. Aren't we supposed to grow up and move on to other teachers, other schools? Isn't the goal of a hospital, after competent treatment, to have the patient discharged, independent and self-sufficient? Isn't it only natural for a child to grow, learn, and leave his father? And shouldn't a father be pleased when this happens?

All true, but Our Heavenly Father's goal is different. Yes, like a human father He joys in watching us grow, mature and discover. He is pleased when we use our resources to help others and overcome obstacles. He longs for us to be fulfilled and at peace. But here's the catch: God the Father knows that this can only take place through Him, with Him, and in Him. To attempt to achieve these ends without Him, to strike out on our own in uncharted waters, is to guarantee unhappiness, failure, and ultimately, death. Take a look at the toddler screaming and struggling against his parent's grip as he tries to cross the busy intersection without help. Check out the kid who insists that he doesn't need a seatbelt because there doesn't appear to be any danger. Or the buddy that figures, *Hey, what are the odds that this could actually lead to a pregnancy?* I can't even imagine how foolish our cries for "freedom" must look to our heavenly Father...

As I slipped from arrogant youth to early manhood I saw the stakes only get higher. Help on a math problem became help taking care of a foster baby. How to spoon out cookie dough became how to spoon out money for a mortgage payment. Tips on a video game were now tips on holding a relationship together. And at some point along the way I've actually figured out that so long as I breathe on this earth, I am in a survival situation, and if I plan on navigating these waters, the cry for help starts now, and the SOS transmission doesn't get turned off until my Father greets me at home port.

Discussion:

1. How do we know when it is time to send a distress call to God?
2. In practical terms, what does it mean to "pray without ceasing?" (1 Thessalonians 5:16-18)
3. Is it possible to rely on God too much? How do we balance the idea of using our God-given

talents to get things done with relying on God to get things done for us?

4. If we already have a rescuer and comforter by our side, why should we continue to cry out for help?

5. Was there ever a time in your life that you cried out to God for help and felt like your signal was too weak or misinterpreted?

6. What are the lifeboats people set up in their life?

7. Why do we equate crying for help as a sign of failure? How can we be leaders of our home, community and country if we are constantly crying for help?

Quotes for Reflection:

1. "Faith transcends reason. It is when the horizon is the darkest and human reason is beaten down to the ground that faith shines brightest and comes to the rescue." Gandhi

2. "Every obnoxious act is a cry for help." Zig Ziglar

3. "The Lord had been very gracious, and spoke peace to me in the time of my distress, and I now most ungratefully turned again to folly; at times I felt sharp reproof, but I did not get low enough to cry for help." John Woolman

4. "When you're drowning, you don't say 'I would be incredibly pleased if someone would have the foresight to notice me drowning and come and help me,' you just scream." John Lennon

Scripture for Reflection:

1. Habakkuk 1:2. It is human to want an instant answer to our cries for help, but the fact is that help arrives according to a rescuer with greater knowledge than our own.
2. Luke 22:41-44. Christ presents us with the example of how a true survivor cries for help
3. Psalm 18:1-17. Our cries for help will elicit a mighty response.

IV

IDENTIFY THE MISSION

Charlie Mike: in the Vietnam era military, radio-speak for "Continue the Mission."

—LTC Leonard B. Scott

What if you were told you had to prepare for a worst-case survival scenario: crash-landing into a remote region of the globe? It could be a desert, the arctic, a jungle, a mountaintop, the ocean…wherever, so be prepared for anything. You will likely be injured. You will be alone. Your supplies, at best, will be what you can fit into your business vest. Oh yes, in addition to all the environmental hazards, there will be a group of trained killers intent on hunting you down and capturing you for the purposes of torture and painful public execution.

This is the exact situation that pilots of the United States military must be prepared for, and in order to do so they attend a rigorous period of training known as SERE: survival, escape, resistance, and evasion. Browse through one of their training manuals and you will find a host of practical survival skills: navigation, shelter building, plant identification, signaling, first-aid, and so forth. In addition, many other factors are approached:

psychology, sociopolitical factors, environment, communication, to name just a few. But which one is most important? Which one would you teach first? SERE chooses to begin with the most important element of any military operation: mission. Every decision, every priority revolves around this one simple factor: identify and accomplish the Mission. Situations, circumstances, resources, terrain…these may all change, but above everything else is the mission. And what is the mission for a downed airman? Maintain life. Maintain honor. Return to friendly forces.

Naval aviator Jim Stockdale never forgot the mission. Shot down in North Vietnam in 1965, he was captured and thrown into the infamous "Hanoi Hilton" prison camp. He was brutally beaten and tortured, locked in a six foot by six foot cell with nothing but leg irons and a tin cup, fed one meal of rice per day, and routinely tortured. His shoulders were wrenched from their sockets, his bones shattered. He was exposed to death and torture on a regular basis, and the only way to survive was to focus on the mission: maintain life.

Commander Stockdale was the senior POW in North Vietnam and therefore everything he did, everything he said, would be held as an example by his fellow prisoners of war. In the military, you look to your commander to be the example under all circumstances. The North Vietnamese torturers knew this, and they were calculating in their cruelty; if they could break Jim, others would quickly follow. Stockdale is told to make a propaganda speech on film. He resists the only way he can, by slicing his scalp open with a razor blade.

They try again later and Jim bashes his own face in with a stool; he refuses to be a "poster boy" for the enemy. He coordinates secret messages of encouragement amongst his fellow prisoners. He and other "hard-core" prisoners are transferred to a harsher location. When told that fellow prisoners were dying under torture because of him, he slits his own wrists rather than submit to his captors' demands. The message is clear: Jim will do nothing to betray the trust of his country and his comrades: Maintain honor.

Jim Stockdale is held in captivity for a period of seven years. Let that sink in for a minute. Think about all that has happened in the last seven years of your life, all the "missions" that you've been given. I'm guessing that few of us can really grasp the magnitude of being separated from loved ones, country, and even the simplest of comforts for such a period of time. What would that do to a person? To a marriage? To your faith? At what point would you simply break down and die of physical neglect and emotional despair? Jim saw this happen all around him, and his captors made sure to remind him that, somehow, each tragic death of a comrade was Commander Stockdale's own fault. Yet, through it all, as year faded into year, Jim never lost sight of the final aspect of his mission: return to friendly forces.

On February 12, 1973, Commander Jim Stockdale was released from captivity. For the next thirty- plus years he continued to receive accolades and serve in a plethora of leadership positions until, in 2005 he succumbed to Alzheimer's disease and was released from earthly captivity. Mission accomplished. Pursue the mission.

Reflection

When I first read the mission statement for downed airmen I was struck by its similarity to the mission of a Christian. Maintain life. Maintain honor. Return to friendly forces. What a powerful analogy of what we ought to be focused on in our quest for spiritual survival!

There is a Latin expression: *Dum vita est spes est,* which translates to, "While there is life, there is hope." It doesn't take a Bible scholar or a degree in theology to figure out that the first mission of a Christian is to live, to live with a sense of hope, and to seek life of the eternal kind. How does one do this? Well, here is where Christianity differs from any other religion. Eternal life is not achieved through a series of good deeds, through a meritorious life, through self-improvement, or through a series of reincarnations and revelations. The only way to eternal life is through God, made flesh, that He might die, that we might live.

Jesus is constantly referring to Himself as the path to eternal life, and indeed, to life itself. He is the bread of life. He is the light of life. He has the words of eternal life. He is the resurrection and the life. And not only is Christ the wellspring of eternal life, He desires us all to share in it. Everything in Scripture points to Christ as being the way to life, indeed, the only way to life. This is a critical point for the spiritual survivor: in order to save your life, you must be willing to lose it

(Luke 9:24). Some might refer to this as being "born again." Sometimes we focus on Christ's example of laying down His life that others may live. Other times we meditate on the Lord's ability to raise the dead. However you wish to think of it, never stray from the truth of the gospel: we are called to live and live with the hope of eternal life through Christ.

Running parallel to the first part of our mission statement lies the second: maintain honor. We dare not call ourselves Christians: followers of Christ, without living an honorable life. Jesus lays it out clearly for us: Be perfect, therefore, as my Heavenly Father is perfect (Matthew 5:48). This is the standard we are called to, and although we recognize the futility of reaching this goal outside of Christ, we also recognize how foolish it would be to lower the standard or disregard Christ's expectations for us.

We don't hear the word honor used much in modern society. It seems like some outdated concept reserved for medieval knights, or samurai warriors. If you look it up, you will find definitions that talk about being fair, noble, honest and trustworthy. Hasn't God planted the meaning of these words in our hearts, and don't we recognize when we are living up to these standards, just as we recognize when we have fallen short? Let's not complicate the matter or fool ourselves; we generally know what the right thing to do is (or to paraphrase Davy Crockett: "Figure out what's right, then do it.").

Every time our words, actions, thoughts and deeds are "Christ-like," we are in a very real sense, maintaining honor. We have been given the ultimate example, the ultimate teacher, and this teacher admonishes us: "Why do you call me, 'Lord, Lord,' and not do what I say?" (Luke 6:46). Do you want to maintain honor under all circumstances? Be associated with and hold favor with Jesus. Call Him "Lord, Lord." Then do as He says. Figure out what's right, then do it.

But let's not kid ourselves, we will fall short. Be perfect? Follow Christ? Do as He says? I have yet to live a day in my adult life that has me adhering to this ultimate honor code. I stray. I wander. Even worse, I deliberately and ambitiously choose a different path. Yes, sometimes I crash-land into enemy territory, but far more often I consciously and casually stroll across the enemy border for a prolonged visit.

Enter part three of our mission statement: return to friendly forces. Look around you. Listen to the news. Examine your soul. Are you in the midst of friendly territory? I can only speak for myself, but far too often the answer is no. The prison I'm in is just as real, just as confining, and ultimately, just as torturous as the one encountered by Commander Stockdale. The difference is, I've chosen this prison, I've too often made my own cell. The question now is: How do I escape? How do I return to friendly forces?

When Christ was being tempted in the prison of the desert (Matthew 4), He experienced much of what we experience: lack of material comfort, the presence of the enemy, temptation, confusing advice and a warping of God's word for selfish ends. Yet through it all we see Christ triumph as He focuses on the mission that God the Father has given Him. And when Christ overcomes the trials of the enemy, He is ready to begin His public ministry by issuing to us our first order of business: repent.

The steps to repentance are the steps to survival. Acknowledge the crisis. Choose life. Send out a distress signal. Continue the mission. Or in the more familiar words of the Church: admit you are a sinner. Recognize God's ability and longing to forgive us. Ask for forgiveness through the blood of the lamb. Go, and sin no more. When we do this we are fulfilling the final part of the survivor's mission statement. We have returned to friendly forces. Whether we choose to remain there or choose to stray back into enemy control is a choice entirely up to us.

Discussion:

1. Have you clearly identified your mission in life? State it.
2. What kind of training are you undergoing in order to accomplish your mission?
3. What is the number one obstacle preventing you from carrying out your mission?
4. Does our mission in life change with circumstances?
5. Think of a real example from your life when you were given the choice to maintain honor. What choice did you make?
6. Who are the friendly forces in your life? Who are the enemy forces?

7. Does your mission statement call for you to go behind enemy lines? What is your plan to survive, escape, resist and evade?

Quotes for Reflection:

1. "Here is the test to find out whether your mission on earth is finished. If you're alive, it isn't." Richard Bach
2. "The battle lines are drawn and there is no middle ground...the only way the terrorists can win is if we lose our nerve and abandon the mission." G.W. Bush
3. "It is a different kind of war where you cannot see the enemy, and there is no front line but nonetheless, this is an entirely real threat..." Sergei Ivanov

Scripture for Reflection:

1. Luke 4:18-19. Christ's mission statement
2. Matthew 28:18-20. Our mission statement.

V

ASSESS THE ENVIRONMENT

The environment is everything that isn't me.

—Albert Einstein

Assess the environment? The dozen or so teenagers paused in response to my question. Some of them let their backpacks slump off aching shoulders. Others just collapsed onto the moist moss of the rainforest floor. They were beyond the point of faking enthusiasm. I smiled. This was the point where I would find out who my leaders were…

We were in the Hoh Rainforest located on the Olympic Peninsula of Washington State. It was a land of prehistoric conifers, drenched in moss and surrounded by enormous ferns. The air was chilly and damp with constant moisture. In every direction one looked there was a feeling of deep antiquity; it seemed a very real possibility that great beasts from the Jurassic era lurked nearby, waiting to be rediscovered by apprehensive eyes.

It was day two of a wilderness training program for camp counselors. Many of my young charges were in reasonable shape, optimistic and eager to learn.

This was good, because most of them had never been through a wilderness experience more intense than a cub scout overnight, and now I was asking them to make critical survival decisions. I rephrased my still-unanswered question: I want you to look around and assess your environment. Another long pause. Then, tentatively, like the dripping of rain off the forest leaves, the answers began to flow.

"That stream nearby will attract mosquitoes at sunset."

"Yes, but it is also a good source of drinking water."

"We can use that pine tree sap as a fire starter."

"True, but we also need to be careful not to let it get on our climbing ropes."

"Those dead branches overhead could be dangerous if it gets windy."

"Good point; those same conditions have also given us some fine firewood for tonight." Environment can help or hinder. Our first lesson: *nature is neutral.*

"We could throw our food sack over that branch to keep it safe from bears, but how can we throw a rope that high?"

"I think this is flint, can't we start a fire with flint?"

"I read that you should sleep in a hammock to keep bugs off you at night. Does anyone know how to make a hammock?"

Our next lesson: *experience frames our options.*

"Let's make sure everyone knows where the latrine is now while it's still light out."

"I can mark west with this branch by seeing where the sun sets."

"Turn your boots upside down and set them on these sticks so critters don't try to snuggle up in them tonight."

"What's that noise? Oh, just another frog."

Another good lesson: *knowledge dispels fear.*

"I think we can clear these rocks out and pitch a tent here."

"This old stump would make a good cook table."

"If we gather up some of those dead branches, we could make some bough mattresses."

Lesson four: *observe reality; envision possibility.*

Nobody has worked up a sweat or burned many calories, but there is already the feeling of great accomplishment. We are excited about the resources around us. We are excited to begin transforming this previously unknown landscape into an overnight resort. A group of weary kids had sat down in a hostile wilderness. Twenty minutes later, a group of motivated young survivors arose in an environment rich in possibility. They had learned a valuable lesson about survival, one that I hoped they would take with them back to their urban lives, and one that I hoped they would embrace spiritually as well: assess the environment.

Reflection

In the previous chapter we talked about pursuing a mission, how every survivor must establish priorities and never lose track of the larger goal. Now we need to assess our environment. Why? Because to a large degree, the circumstances of environment will either help us or hinder us in accomplishing our mission.

Let's start with our first lesson: nature is neutral. By that we mean that it is not a benevolent "mother," serenely embracing her "children" and encouraging us to live in harmony with her perfectly balanced ways. This is the mindset of those people you see trying to get the bears at Yellowstone to eat peanut butter out of their kid's hands even as they take snapshots from the minivan. This is a trap that many well-meaning people fall into: nature worship. Appreciate the spirituality of God's handiwork, and be respectful of His creation, yes. But never blur the worship of Creator with the worship of creation.

Conversely, nature is not an evil, vindictive force, out to punish those who dare tread along its pathways. Mosquitoes aren't chortling gleefully as they buzz about your face at two in the morning. Clouds don't cleverly wait until you've changed into your only dry socks before they unleash a downpour upon you. Nature is not "out to get you." This is easy for me to write in the comfort of my living room, much more difficult to acknowledge in the wilderness. When my brother-in-law was in Africa he encountered a man who had just had his leg eaten off by a crocodile. My priest lost his dear brother to the venom of a snake. A friend of mine saw his house torn asunder by a tornado, even while his neighbor's house remained unscathed. At that moment in time, did they consider nature to be neutral? I'm not sure I would. This is why it is so important to reflect upon this during a time of calm and tranquility. Whether soaking up rays on the glorious sands of a tropical beach or fighting off a swarm of bald-faced hornets, you can't take it personally. Nature doesn't. Nature is neutral.

Our next point: experience frames our options. This simply means that skills, knowledge and wisdom that we do or don't have will determine the choices available to us. In the woods this might mean experience with fire starting will determine who is sleeping comfy warm and who is doing jumping jacks at midnight trying not to freeze to death. In our walk with Christ this might mean experience with establishing relationships or the skill of sharing Scripture will determine how effectively we minister to others. We ought to always be seeking to improve our skills and widen our knowledge base, but we must be honest about our ability levels, especially in a survival situation. Far too many people have slipped into crisis mode because they underestimated their environment or overestimated their abilities. Now go back and read that last line again.

Our third point: knowledge dispels fear. To the wilderness survivor this might mean confidence in one's knowledge of navigation. For the urban survivor, knowledge of how to talk one's self out of a violent altercation. For the spiritual survivor, knowledge that Jesus has a personal interest in our well-being and commands a legion of heavenly hosts to make sure that we are protected from whatever snares the devil has laid for us. The more we know about Christ's love for us, the greater knowledge we have of God's mercy, the easier it becomes for us to set fear aside and replace it with faith, and for a person in a survival situation there is nothing of greater value than faith.

Our final point in assessing the environment: observe reality; envision possibility. You must see the reality but seek the possibilities. You must be simultaneously realistic and optimistic, acknowledging problems even while envisioning how they might be overcome. It is this mindset that frequently means the difference between life and death in a crisis. I am reminded of the family trapped in the desert who survived on crayons and radiator water. Or the man who amputated his own hand with a pocket knife to escape the pinning effect of a boulder and certain dehydration. Or the girl who convinced a convicted rapist and murderer that surrender was a better option than slashing her with a butcher knife. All of these survivors would have been foolish to have ignored the reality of their environment; all would have perished had they not gone beyond reality to envision a possibility.

Because of our relationship with the Holy Spirit we are able to assess our environment not with the limitations of our own experience, knowledge and vision, but with the unlimited potential of our heavenly Paraclete. Browse through Scripture and you will find this a very reassuring thought: Through God all things are possible. I can do all things through Christ. My God shall provide all my needs. Angels shall attend me. We shall be provided with an advocate. When we embrace the reality of this, our own limitations diminish, our creativity and boldness increase, and we can assess the possibilities of our environment in much broader terms.

You want to survive under any circumstances? Accept the gift of the Holy Spirit and the power that entails; then assess the environment.

Discussion:

1. Is it possible to assess a spiritual environment? Can it be done with your senses, or does it require spiritual senses?
2. Do you agree with the idea that nature is neutral? Is Creation neutral?
3. Think of a time when you overestimated your abilities or underestimated the environment. Try to come up with one example from the physical realm and one from the spiritual realm. Lessons learned?
4. Knowledge dispels fear. What is the bottom line knowledge we must have in order to dispel fear in any situation? If we have this knowledge, then why do we still fear?
5. Would you consider yourself more a pessimist, realist or optimist? Which mindset seems most useful for physical survival? Spiritual survival? Which seems best for a Christian mindset?
6. How does our third point-knowledge dispels fear- relate to the scripture passage: "perfect love casts out fear?" (1John4:18).

Quotes for Reflection:

1. "Man must cease attributing his problems to his environment and learn again to exercise his will-his personal responsibility in the areas of faith and morals." Albert Schweitzer
2. "The first step toward success is taken when you refuse to be a captive of the environment in which you first find yourself." Mark Caine
3. "Some people aren't used to an environment where excellence is expected." Steven Jobs

Scripture for Reflection:

1. Genesis 1:31. God Himself assesses the environment
2. Genesis 3:17. And a reassessment as humans impact their environment
3. Luke 14:28-29. One who does not first assess the environment will be derided as a fool.
4. 1Corinthians10:13. He will always provide you with the necessary resources.

VI

DECISION TO MOVE

Those who do not move do not notice their chains.

—Rosa Luxemburg

In a crisis scenario, survival itself can hinge upon the decision of whether to move or to stay put. Think of a soldier being pressed by enemy fire. Think of a hiker injured in a remote wilderness. Or think of Paul O'Connor.

Paul grew up in the heartland of America, an average guy, working a farm to support a family. I can imagine him in 1935, staring out across a sorry looking wheat crop, his son playing in the parched soil by his side. The boy seems to blend in with the lanky, burnished wheat, slightly bent, thirsting for a better life. Five years old. It's easy to remember his age because the last time it rained was on the day of his birth. Paul smiles a grim smile, remembering all the teasing he gave his wife about how it was the day that "the waters broke." The boy cocks his tousled head and stares curiously at his father's smile…Smiles, rain and wheat; all seemed a rarity in those days.

Even in normal times the Midwest is a land of harsh extremes, but now in the midst of the Great Dustbowl, nature seems intent on shattering all records. The cold snap of 1934, with temperatures refusing to rise above zero for a month, sometimes bottoming out at sixty below. In that month Paul had tried to help a neighbor right an overturned bobsled, entrapped in a four foot snowdrift. The missing fingers on his right hand were permanent testament to what such temperatures could do to human flesh.

The summer of 1935. The thermometer registered 120 degrees before it burst into shattered glass and mercury. That was the time that the chickens wandered about with their beaks opened skyward, when the pigs roasted to death in their own skin. That was the time of the grasshopper plague. They were locusts, three to four inches long, arriving in swarms of biblical proportion. They devoured everything in their path: crops, paint off the fence, everything. His little girl left a doll in the front yard and the creatures actually ate the dress off the doll's body. Kerosene and chickens could kill only so many of the winged hoard, and, as country folk were fond of saying, for every one killed, a thousand more came to the funeral.

And of course, the foreclosures. This seemed the worst tragedy of all, because it was a disaster spawned not by nature, but by the greed and short-sightedness of Man. Broken neighbors begging from broken banks propped up by a broken government. Broken promises all around. Paul saw one in four of his neighbors flee the county in hopes of a better life. What must have been his thoughts? How does one decide whether to flee or entrench?

It is a wall of blackness, a unimaginable storm of dust stretching from horizon to horizon, eight thousand feet high, and approaching with the speed and fury of a freight train. Within its swirling, roiling mass is enough electricity to run New York City for a year, charging the atmosphere so much that every strand of barbed wire on his property is sending off angry blue sparks. It's 6 PM on April 14th, 1935. History books today refer to it as Black Sunday.

Paul reached to grab his son, but the air is so charged with static electricity created by the dust and dry air that the shock upon contact literally hurled them both to the ground. Scrambling to his feet, he yelled for his son to run to the house as fast as he could, even as Paul raced for the barn. Paul hoped to save the livestock, cover their noses with wet grain sacks. But now he felt the black dust whipping against his skin. It burns. Funny how soft and fine the dust feels when settled on the ground; now it tears his flesh and burns like fire.

He glanced desperately around the barn looking for some grain sacks. Then he remembered that his wife used the last of them up to sew a new pair of pants for their son. He is now smacked full in the face by choking, furious clouds of death. You can't survive sixty seconds in conditions like this. He cursed silently as he left the animals, knowing full well what will happen to them in the storm. When they are butchered in the morning black sand will steadily pour forth from their mouth, stomachs and lungs. Paul cannot focus on this, he can only grab the guide rope tied between barn and house and stumble toward his loved ones.

He staggered through the door, his wife quickly re-covering the door crack with damp rags. Every crack, every nail hole in the house had been sealed and resealed for years now in an effort to keep the invasive dust from entering. The dry air warps and shrinks the wooden boards, and every morning when the house is re-swept, they were reminded of the futility of the task. Seven bucket loads of dust.

He cannot make out the kerosene lantern just outside. He cannot see the faces of his family huddled in his arms. The blackness is total. The roof itself, the only thing saving them from death by suffocation, is rising and falling just above, as if the rafters were a great set of ribs, as if he and his family were in the bowels of the great Leviathan of Jonah. Paul is a man of faith, but he is also a man in despair. Is this a test of God? Does God want him to stand firm in this tempest, or is this a harbinger, calling him in preparation to depart? Listening to the creaking and groaning of the wooden frame and the howling of the storm, he imagines what it must have felt like during the first Passover, when the angel of death swept through the country of Egypt and God's people huddled behind flimsy doors and firm promises. Was this a sign? Was he being asked to lead his family out of this barren desert to a land flowing with milk and honey, to a land flowing with opportunity and promise? How could he tell? How can anyone tell? How do you make the decision to move?

Reflection

One of the first decisions that must be made in a crisis is whether to stay put or to move. Most survival manuals will caution against moving unless absolutely necessary. Remaining in one spot makes it easier for rescuers to find you, particularly if you are near a crash site, vehicle, or established camp. Moving about may increase the chances of becoming injured and running into hazardous conditions. Departing a known area might cut you off from established shelter, food and water supplies. Traveling when lost can deplete energy reserves. And constantly moving about might prevent you from creating a substantial shelter.

There are times, however, when moving becomes advantageous, even necessary, for survival. Resources might be too scarce at your present location. Hazardous environmental conditions like flood waters, rock slides or animal life might necessitate travel. Serious illness or injury requiring advanced medical care is another good reason. And finally, being in a location where rescue is unlikely demands the survivor to strike out for a better locale. Clearly, whether to move or stay put must be considered carefully in a physical survival scenario. But we are more concerned with spiritual survival, and from that perspective there can be no doubt: We must make the decision to move.

Skim through the Bible for even a few moments and one thing quickly becomes apparent: God is constantly on the move. From the first verses of Genesis when we hear of the Spirit of God moving across the formless earth, to the last verses of Revelation, where Christ proclaims, I am coming soon, there is a constant movement. Whether it's traveling through large cities like Jerusalem, praying in deserted places, or even traveling along the *Via Dolorosa*, the way of the cross, our most holy example seems to be on a purposeful sojourn. He solemnly assures us that there will be no place to lay His head, like the foxes or the birds of the air. Why is this? Is the Son of Man driven by discontent and a restless spirit? Fear for His life? Seeking the perfect base of operations? Of course not, Christ is constantly on the move because He is fulfilling His mission, and His mission is one of search, rescue and pursuit. The whole nature of a search and rescue action is to go forth, find the victim, and return to safety. This can only be accomplished through purposeful and deliberate movement, and nobody does this better than the Christ.

That's great if you're the Son of God, charged with saving the crestfallen and finding the lost. After all, He's the shepherd, accountable for His flock. But what about the sheep? I thought Scripture says something about God giving rest to the weary; and elsewhere: Be still, and know that I am God; and still elsewhere, let the beloved of the Lord rest secure in him. Isn't the whole benefit of becoming a Christian the idea of rest and contentment?

That's a classic pitfall in spiritual survival, and it stems from the fact that we forget about our own mission statement. Many who are lost in the wilderness, upon escaping from immediate and apparent danger, warp the mission. It is no longer, "Maintain life, maintain honor, return to safety." It becomes, "Now that I'm saved I can relax and multiply my blessings in the land of the enemy." They begin construction of permanent dwellings, maybe plant some crops, perhaps establish permanent relationships with the locals. They feel welcomed, comfortable. Now that they "understand" the "cultural differences" of the "enemy," they realize that the beliefs and lifestyles of these people really aren't that bad. After all, it's all about tolerance and compromise, right?

Insidious, isn't it? Like the Egyptian Jews of old, slavery and hardship in a foreign land actually becomes preferable to an exodus. Well, here's an inconvenient truth: Christ doesn't want us getting too comfortable on this planet. He doesn't want us sinking our spiritual roots deep into secular soil. He doesn't want us to wallow in our personal salvation. The truth is, He wants us to go! Go forth and make disciples of all nations! Go in peace! Go to Him!

We are called to grow, and there can be no growing without going. Rest when we are weary, yes. Receive solace and comfort from our rescuer, of course. But don't think for a second that Christ's rescue mission ended with your personal salvation. Rejoice, refresh, but then make the decision to move.

Discussion:

1. When trials happen, how can we discern if God is using this as a means to tell us it's time to

move on, or if He is testing our faith and wants us to stand fast?

2. What is the difference between a pilgrim and a refugee? Between movement and flight?

3. What lessons can be learned by a refugee that might not be easily learned by the settled person?

4. What would it take to convince you to move several hundred miles from where you currently live?

5. To move suggests change and change suggests growth. Yet, many times we move about, physically or spiritually, without truly changing. Some people bounce dissatisfied from church to church, job to job, relationship to relationship with no real growth or change occurring. Think of an example from your life where movement did not result in change and growth.

Quotes for reflection:

1. "It is only through labor and painful effort, by grim energy and resolute courage, that we move on to better things." Theodore Roosevelt

2. "How do geese know when to fly to the sun? Who tells them the seasons? How do we, humans know when it is time to move on? As with the migrant birds, so surely with us, there is a voice within if only we would listen to it, that tells us certainly when to go forward into the unknown." Elisabeth Kubler-Ross

3. "A tree does not move unless there is wind." Nigerian proverb
4. "Nothing happens until something moves." Sir John Denham

Scripture for reflection:

1. Exodus 14: 13-15. God clarifies when it is time to move on. We must not remain rigid to our own plans.
2. Numbers 16:23-26. There are times to move from evil influence.
3. 1Cor 15: 58. And there are times to remain still

PART II:

SURVIVAL SKILLS

Principles are great, but without practical application they remain just that: principles. In Part II we take a look at what can be termed, "traditional" survival skills, those which you might expect to find in any survival manual. *I encourage you to practice these skills under competent supervision: many is the time that practicing a survival skill has resulted in triggering an actual survival situation.* That being said, practice is the key to performance, be it in the physical realm or the spiritual. Like Part I, embedded in most every line of Part II is a spiritual metaphor. Do not become so engrossed in the skill that you miss the true lesson behind it. The discussion questions and scripture passages that follow each sub-section will hopefully help you avoid this snare.

VII

READ THE SIGNS AND PLOT A COURSE: LESSONS FROM NAVIGATION

I've never been lost. I have been powerfully confused for three or four days at a time, however.

—Daniel Boone

As Christians, we must never forget that we are strangers in a foreign land, and I would be lying if I said that our pilgrimage will be an easy one or that the inhabitants of this land will always have our best interests in mind. As a matter of fact, the more I think of the pain that life presents us, the more appealing is the idea of building up my own personal stronghold and waiting for the final trumpet call to announce that Dad is calling us home. Unfortunately, that's not our mission, is it? We are called to move. But if I have to move across potentially dangerous and unfamiliar terrain, it might be helpful to acquire and hone some navigation skills. At its core, navigation is a very simple three-tiered task:

knowing where you are, knowing where you want to be, and knowing the nature of the routes in order to proceed from point A to point B. Those who ignore these tasks will soon discover that there are an amazing number of ways to lose your way…

Read the map: A reliable map is a pretty amazing thing. It gives you perspective. It allows you to plan for the future. It presents options. It gives a sense of distance. It outlines the works of Man and the works of nature. And it reminds you that no matter how alien this terrain might seem to you, you are not the first to traverse its pathways.

A map is meant to be read, but not in the same way that one might read ordinary text. You cannot focus on a small area and expect to understand the lay of the land. You must understand symbolism as well as literal words. You have to apply the knowledge to your given situation, but you cannot change what the map says based on personal goals, preconceived notions, or a desire to make things easier. Other tools, like a protractor or compass, are often useful in interpreting data. And of course, all the advantages of studying a map are useless if you doubt the reliability of the map-maker. Now go back and re-read this section replacing the word, "map" with "Bible."

Discussion:

1. In what ways do you use Scripture as a map for your life? Be specific.

2. Reading a map does not get us to where we want to go; it merely offers us a viable route. So too, with Scripture. How have you taken a biblical principle and used it to further your pilgrimage?

Scripture for Reflection:

1. Luke 6:49. Reading a map is not enough, you must apply what is set before you.
2. James 1:22-25. Learn to use a compass:
   Then put your trust in it. To many, a compass is a mystical device: just go wherever the arrow points. Unfortunately, such people don't understand that even though a compass needle points stalwartly North, this may not be the direction you ought to go. They don't understand that metal, electric currents and magnets can create false compass readings. And in never learning how to use it, a compass becomes not a tool for a survival but simply another burden to be carried.

Contrast this with those who have studied and mastered the principles of compass work. They understand declination diagrams, back azimuths and triangulation. They have practiced and studied, and have been rewarded with confidence in their silent guide. It can be trusted over gut feelings and emotions. It is more powerful than our misconceptions. It is not influenced by peers or popular opinions. For them, a compass is an invaluable tool for survival.

But remember this: do not fixate on the compass; it merely points to the destination. It is a signpost. Do not fixate on churches or saints, theology or miracles (often referred to as "signs"); such things merely point the way to what, or Who, is truly important.

Discussion:

1. God has given everyone the compass of conscience (c.f. Romans 1:20). How can we train ourselves to read this survival tool?
2. A compass, though useful, can be swayed by outside influences. What are the influences that sway our conscience?

Scripture for Reflection:

1. Exodus 13: 21-22. One heck of a compass!
2. Proverbs 1: 5-7. Compass training.

Memorize landmarks and way points: On any given route, there are usually a series of landmarks we can use to mark progress and instill confidence that we are indeed on the right path. It could be a natural feature, such as an unusual rock formation or distinctive tree, or it could be a reference created by people: a trail marker or abandoned railroad tracks, perhaps. Both sources of information can prove valuable, so do not fixate on one at the expense of the other.

There may be long periods of time when there seems to be nothing to either confirm or deny the correctness of our sojourn. It is at times like this when it might pay off to change your perspective. Crouch down or look skyward, focus in on a detail or gaze broadly at a general vista. Bear in mind which landmarks exhibit true permanence and which ones are subject to change with the ravages of time. Combine what you know to be true with what your senses report and you ought to have a pretty good sense of whether or not you are on the right path.

Discussion:

1. What landmark events in your life have provided you with assurance of being on the right path?
2. What is an example of a way point that once helped to guide you, but is now no longer as useful in doing so? It could be a person, institution, circumstances, etc.

Scripture for Reflection:

1. Genesis 28:16-18; Exodus 12:17. Spiritual landmarks ought to be established.

Look back on occasion: Sometimes the most valuable way you can confirm whether you are moving forward on the right path is to look backward. By keeping two stationary objects lined up you can prevent the natural inclination to drift with changes in terrain (Scripture speaks of the reliability of two witnesses). You can get perspective on changes in altitude and gauge travel speed. It can even serve to bolster your morale by reminding you of how far you've come. And of course, it can help you confirm your way back to a known point should you be forced to backtrack.

But be careful. There are pitfalls for the traveler who becomes obsessed with looking at what was instead of what will be (c.f. Luke 9:62). To the one that continually looks over the shoulder can come paranoia, doubt, and regret. It can produce a wasteful lurch in your stride and direction. It can serve as an unwelcome reminder of how little you have accomplished and how far you must go. Not to mention, it's a sure way to stumble over the immediate obstacle to your front.

Discussion:

1. Reflect on a time when looking at the past has helped you. Hurt you.
2. How can you look to the past for guidance without getting bogged down by regret, guilt or pride?

Scripture for Reflection:

1. Deuteronomy 4:9. We are called to not only remember what we have learned but to pass God's lessons on to our children.
2. Luke 22:19. In looking back, we look to our own future.

Take the high road: Anyone who has participated in the sport of orienteering or geocaching quickly learns the axiom: Run the Ridges. A ridgeline is that narrow piece of real estate that connects one piece of high ground to the next, and when everything is said and done, it is generally the best path to pursue. Ridges generally avoid sudden changes in elevation. They are usually home to roads, pathways, railroad tracks...in short, ideal pathways to travel. Because they are elevated, they offer commanding views of surrounding terrain. They avoid the pitfalls of low level terrain: swamplands, heavy undergrowth, and areas prone to rock slide or avalanche. Ridges make it easier for rescuers to spot you and for you to spot them.

But taking the high road isn't always easy. It may be tempting to follow a route that is more direct. A ridgeline is often narrow. You are exposed to the elements. If walking through enemy territory, the enemy can clearly see you and pursue. And sometimes the high road leads you across terrain you don't want to traverse, leaving you in a place you don't want to be in. Perhaps there are other paths that are more rational, more comfortable. These are all valid considerations when crossing physical space, but in the spiritual realm you cannot fool yourself into validating compromise: though narrow it may be, take the high road.

Discussion:

1. Taking the high road silhouettes your presence to enemy forces. Is it ever okay to take the

"lower road" as a means of avoiding detection? For example, remaining quiet about your faith at the start of a relationship? Hanging out a bar or strip club to witness to those who might never hear the gospel message?

2. How can taking the high road facilitate better communication from on high?

Scripture for Reflection:

1. Matthew 7: 13-14. The road is narrow.
2. Proverbs 15: 24. Survival lies on the high road.

Interpret the signs: Even in the most remote wilderness, signs will be revealed to those with the wisdom to interpret them: the sound of a stream, the smell of domestic animals, the feeling of an isotherm on your cheek, the taste of sea spray, the popping of your ears as barometric pressure and altitude change, the scent of climactic vegetation, or even the absence of a particular phenomena, can all suggest where we are and the path we are taking.

We are a generation that demands signs. I have been on "rustic" hiking trails where it seems like every third tree is spray painted with an obnoxious trail marker or fluorescent sign post. We even place talking computers on our dash boards that remind us in a sultry female voice to "turn left in twenty yards." And when the signs we expect to guide us are absent, there is a feeling of confusion, even anger, as if the one who posted the signs has let us down. More than likely, the signs are right in front of us. We simply refuse to change our mindset in order to see them or have failed to hone the skills necessary to interpret them. If being "found" is important to us, we must learn to interpret the signs.

Discussion:

1. Think in terms of relationship (with Christ, spouse, etc). Are there signs being revealed to you that you tend to ignore or overlook? Why?

2. Pacific Islanders have trained themselves to navigate by the froth of ocean waves; Inuits by the crusting structure of ice formations: subtle signs, indeed, yet well worth the effort in a survival situation. As a Christian, how can you train yourself to interpret spiritual signs? Why is interpreting signs not enough?

Scripture for Reflection:

1. Matthew 16:1-4. Christ tells us it is a wicked man who demands miraculous signs, a foolish man who demands signs he cannot interpret.

2. Genesis 1: 14. From the very beginning God has used Creation to provide us with useful signs.

Learn from those who have gone before you: Maps, compasses, GPS systems…these are all wonderful tools for navigation; but there is nothing more valuable than an experienced guide. Whether it be the streets of New York or the basin of the Amazon, one man's hostile wilderness is another man's back yard, and in a hostile wilderness how I long for someone who has walked before me, who can point out the dangers and pitfalls, who can teach me the value of local resources, who can show me how to obtain sustenance and shelter, and provide counsel at the crossroads!

Even without the physical presence of a guide, we can still be guided by the impact of those who have gone before us. Everything in God's creation leaves a footprint: the wind-blown ridges of a sand dune, the scratches of a chipmunk on a rotting log, the leaning of a tree trunk toward sunlight, but there is nothing quite as distinct and reassuring as a human footprint. It assures us that others have gone through what we are about to encounter. It gives us confidence that we, too, can make it to the other side. It reminds us that we are never really alone.

Of course, Jesus is our ultimate guide and example, and I never cease to give Him thanks and glory for showing us the way. I am also grateful for the example of the saints, who, though imperfectly human, give further example of what it means to follow God through a wilderness.

Discussion:

1. What is the danger of placing total confidence in a spouse/friend/institution as a guide?
2. We all leave a spiritual footprint on our journey. What markers do you hope to establish for those who may follow in your path?

Scripture for Reflection:

1. Proverbs 6:20-22. God provides us with guides in a myriad of forms.
2. Matthew 7:15; 23: 16-24. But beware of false guides.

VIII

SPARKS, FUEL AND FLAMES: LESSONS FROM FIRE

"I have come to bring fire on the earth, and how I wish it were already kindled!"

—Christ

Ask people what kind of skills they would expect to find in a survival manual and more than likely their first response will be, "fire-making." There is something about the ability to summon a fire that transcends time, place and culture. It is what separates us from the animals and, in many mythologies, that which draws us closer to the divine. It provides us with a plethora of comforts: heat, the ability to cook food, light, purification, protection, guidance and even inspiration (Old colonial expression: "Wood warms us thrice: once when we cut it, once when we burn it, and once when we stare into the comfort of its flames"). And although we can call upon it at will, it is not something we invented or something we claim mastery over, or something we can ignore. In short, it is a wonderful metaphor for the Spirit of God.

Fuel: Every fire begins with, and is distinguished by, its source of fuel. What we feed it will determine its character. It's true that our sources of fuel are limited by the environment, but knowledge, foresight and persistence can provide us with acceptable fuel under an incredible array of situations. I think of famed Antarctic survivor, Ernest Shackleton, who kept his ice-locked crew alive and healthy for months by burning seal blubber. I think of Les Stroud, a.k.a. "Survivorman," who has utilized fuel sources as diverse as duct tape or cough drops. I even remember the time that I kept my simple arctic fire kindled with a steady supply of shelled peanuts and mosquito repellent. Animal dung, bacon grease, pine duff, deodorant, corn chips, chapstick…it's amazing the variety of fuel sources at our disposal.

The character of a fire will be determined by its fuel. Want smoke to preserve food, keep out insects or signal rescuers? Green boughs. Want an extremely hot flame? Oil and water mixture. Long burning, steady heat? Seasoned hardwood. To some degree we can change the nature of the fuel, for example, cutting frizzle sticks, fluffing or splitting to expand surface area, mixing a variety of fuel surfaces, or simply allowing time for wood to dry and cure. And of course, let us not forget a simple axiom of fire-making: if you run out of fuel, even the finest fire will move from distinguished to extinguished.

Discussion:

1. What fuel are you using to feed your spirit? Are there other sources available you have yet to consider?
2. Is it possible to stockpile spiritual fuel for the future? Is there a way you can modify a poor fuel source to make it more productive?
3. Tragedy strikes and you must use your Bible as an emergency fire starter. Which book would you give up first? Which one last? What does this reveal to you?

Scripture for Reflection:

1. 1Kings 18:35-39. Miraculous fuel confirms God's dominance over idolatry
2. Isaiah 44:15-15. Be mindful what you use your fuel to accomplish

Spark: Fire requires a source of heat or "sparking agent" for it to begin. This can occur naturally: lightning strikes, volcanic activity, or even the spontaneous combustion generated by a pile of damp hay. In a survival situation you ought to be cognizant of these agents, not so much as a reliable way to start a fire, but as a potentially hazardous situation to be aware of. We are more interested in reliable sparking agents that can be produced on demand: striking flint to steel, focusing the rays of the sun, friction, and chemical reactions.

Whenever possible, we should keep at least one sparking element on our being; not in a backpack or car trunk, but truly on our being: around your neck or in a pocket. Imagine flicking a windproof lighter or match. Now think of trying to focus the winter sun through a piece of convex ice or making a fire-drill because your gear was lost in a mishap. It can be done, but only with great effort and with prior knowledge and experience. Keep your sparking agent close.

A spark with nothing to ignite is simply a vanity for the eye and a source of heartbreak for the survivor. A spark must be caught, nurtured, and encouraged. This can be done on a piece of charred cloth, bird's nesting, birch bark, or other suitable tinder. From the smallest flame, life can subside, but remember the survivor's adage: Never light a match without also lighting a candle. Catch the spark. Nurture it with the choicest of fuels. Encourage it with the gentlest of breaths.

Discussion:

1. When you are in need of the life-giving comfort of a spiritual flame, who or what is your "sparking agent?"
2. Reflect upon a time in your life when you have been inspired or impassioned from an unexpected sparking agent.

Scripture for Reflection:

1. Luke 12:49. Christ is the ultimate sparking agent.
2. Leviticus 10:1-2 Sparking agents are not toys; play with fire and you will get burned.

Oxygen: Without adequate oxygen a fire can only smolder and char. Such a flame will never reach its potential and will be useful for very little. Uncontrolled oxygen upon a fire will simply serve to extinguish it or create an unintended maelstrom of destruction. Both scenarios can mean death one in crisis, so discretion must be used in "fanning the flames."

When constructing a fire, be aware of wind strength and direction. Arrange your fuel to funnel breezes into the heart of the fire. Use wind blocks and be aware of what unsuspecting gusts might do to your surroundings. A hollow tube of some sort can be used to blow oxygen onto a focused area (just be careful not to inhale while the tube is near the fire!). Squeeze bottles and fans are also useful for keeping your face a safe distance from smoke and flames. Remember that fire burns up, so concentrate your efforts at the base of the fire, perhaps even elevating your tinder source above head level to prevent inhaling smoke and avoiding the need to kneel on damp ground. Pace and intensity are critical when first fanning a fire and your infant flame will be happy to give you feedback on your technique.

In Hebrew, the word "*ruah*" is translated both as "breath" and "spirit" as we see in Genesis when the spirit of God moves across the waters. The two are closely affiliated which is why we say "God bless you" when someone sneezes, and "breathing his last" is synonymous with "giving up his spirit" (Think of God breathing life into Adam and Christ giving up his spirit on the cross). Without the grace of the Holy Spirit in our lives we cannot expect our internal fire to survive.

Discussion:

1. Can you think of a time that the "ruah" of God has fanned a smoldering ember in your life?
2. Reflect upon a time when your "ruah" was either too strong or too weak, resulting in the reduction of another's fire. In other words, how have you been overly zealous or disheartening to those around you?

Scripture for Reflection:

1. 2Timothy 1:6-7. The spirit turns a spark into a flame.
2. John 20:21-23. Christ fans the flames of His disciples.

Mixture: Fuel, Spark, and Oxygen; the fire triangle is complete. So why the heck isn't your fire going? Perhaps for the same reason that throwing yeast, water and flour into a bowl doesn't necessarily produce a loaf of bread: you must have the proper mixture. The best survival fires are the ones where the amount of fuel, spark and oxygen can be readily controlled.

Make sure your fuel is divided into 3 piles: tinder, kindling and fuel. Have these close at hand for use as "fast fuel," but not so close as to present a hazard. Gather more than you think you need. Use a dry piece of fuel as the base for your fire, for example, creating a twig teepee on top of a split piece of seasoned wood. This not only keeps the infant flame from coming into contact with the damp ground, it also give you a head start on igniting a larger fuel source. Arrange the fuel so that it collapses upon itself, thus self-feeding the fire. This can be done in the shape of a log-cabin, a teepee, or a "star" where the extensions of wood can be manually pushed into or away from the fire's heart. Do not add fuel too quickly or haphazardly; this will reduce oxygen and smother your efforts. Have a secondary "spark" ready to go in case your efforts seem about to fail but you are on the brink of success. This might be a lit candle, additional char cloth, or a particularly choice piece of tinder. If your best efforts fail, reflect upon the mixture of your fire triangle and see if you can adjust the "recipe."

Discussion:

1. Consider your "fire triangle" as being your body, mind and spirit. Do you feel these elements to be in a proper mixture in your life?
2. Are there any activities in your life that "self-feed" your fire, simultaneously enriching all sides of the fire triangle?

Scripture for Reflection:

1. Psalm 18:28. God assures the proper mixture to produce good results.
2. Isaiah 42:1-3. Christ is attentive when our spirit grows weak.

Vigilance: There's nothing like the satisfaction of producing a hearty fire, particularly in a survival situation. But this is not the time to grow careless or apathetic; fire requires vigilance. Huddled around your little cook fire it may be hard to imagine an inferno that can outrace a man on horseback without care of what, or who, is consumed in the process. Similarly, it's hard to envision how quickly your mighty bonfire can be reduced to lukewarm ashes. Vigilance is the key.

Never start a fire without the means to put it out. Clear the area of surrounding flammables, including an inspection for roots below and branches above. But also be aware of environmental conditions that might accidently extinguish your fire, such as loose snow, splashing water or wind gusts. Be mindful that the wood you intend for use as fuel might be home to dangerous insects, reptiles or plant life. Do not sleep so close to your fire as to have sparks ignite your clothes or gear. Gather tinder throughout the day and store it in a dry place. If possible, do not wait for nightfall to collect wood. Try to carry a live ember with you if moving to another site. If used for daytime signaling, have a source of green wood, rubber items, or other smoke producers ready for immediate use.

Discussion:

1. Reflect upon a time that you have been burned by a fire of your own making.
2. People speak of being "on fire" for the Lord, only to find themselves weary or disappointed a short time later. How might you "inspect" your spiritual fire to ensure that it is neither in danger of dying or becoming all-consuming?

Scripture for Reflection:

1. James 3:5. The smallest negligence can result in the mightiest conflagration.
2. Proverbs 26:18-19. How like madmen we sometime act.
3. Matthew 25. There is a price for a lack of vigilance.

IX

FILTER, PURIFY AND REFRESH: LESSONS FROM WATER

Water, water every where, nor any drop to drink.

—Samuel T. Coleridge

There are life forms that can survive without oxygen. There are creatures that never see the rays of the sun. There are other beings that can survive the extremes of underwater volcanic vents, radiation-laced chemical baths or toxic goo. But when scientists look for life on other planets or in hyper-extreme environments, there is a given: nothing survives without water. This is as true now as it was thousands of years ago when the Son of God declared Himself to be the water of life and eons before that when life itself began with the Spirit of God hovering over the waters. Water incorporates the bulk of every cell in our bodies, which in turn float in a bath of intercellular water. And if we ignore the physiological need to continually restore and refresh our need for water, we shall surely perish.

Signs of dehydration: Thirst is a universal human experience. It is ironic that we live on a planet predominantly covered with water inside a body predominantly made of water, yet, we experience thirst throughout our entire life. The signs and symptoms of dehydration are known to all, because to some degree we have experienced them: the dry mouth, decreased urination that becomes dark colored, irritability and a fixation for water. This is where it begins, but most Americans have not experienced dehydration at the life-threatening level: sunken eyes, the inability to sweat, low blood pressure and a rapid heartbeat, delirium, fevers, seizures, unconsciousness, and eventually, death.

Discussion:

1. Are we more likely to recognize dehydration in others or in ourselves? Why? Are we more likely to recognize "spiritual dehydration" in others or ourselves? Why?
2. How would you describe the signs of spiritual dehydration? The symptoms?

Scripture for Reflection:

1. John 4:13-14. We need not fear spiritual dehydration.
2. John 19:28. In a touching display of His humanity, Christ Himself thirsts.

Sources: Where does one find water in a survival situation? The human body, doing essentially nothing but being, requires two to three quarts of water each day. Throw in some sun, exertion, and survival stresses and the amount increases dramatically.

Perhaps the first consideration ought to be how we can preserve the water already in us. Be still. Only move if it is critical to survival. Lie down on cool soil. Sleep. If you don't have to talk, don't; you're only losing water to the atmosphere, and for that matter, breathe through your nose instead of your mouth. Cover your body to protect it from the drying effects of sun and wind. Don't forget to cover your head. Remember that digestion requires water, so balance the advantage of eating food, even moist food, with the disadvantage of digestive requirements. Avoid food that is excessively salty, spicy or hot. Of course, if you have that option you are probably not in a true survival situation anyway...

What about rationing water? Should you consume, say, eight ounces a day, knowing that you will run out before obtaining more? Experts disagree on this one, and I don't claim to be an expert in this area (classic definition of an expert: an "ex" is a has-been and a "spurt" is a drip under pressure). I guess my line of thinking is this: Don't "ration" to the point that you become "irrational." It doesn't do you any good to conserve water to the point that you are make foolish decisions and thereby decrease the chances of survival. I'd hate to die from stupidity caused by dehydration only to be found with water left in my canteen...

In your quest for water, think about sources that are higher up (less likely to be contaminated from upstream sources) and running (again, less likely to contain contaminants). The planet is something like 70 percent covered with water, your body is 90 percent water, plants, animals, and even rocks often contain water, and the air itself generally contains water. If you can't find running water, your next choice is standing water. Look for depressions or rock formations that might collect rain water. Follow the paths left by animals, particularly those that lead downhill. Dig into dark or moist soil or soil rich in plant life.

Finally, if surface or shallow water is unavailable, you might have to turn to other sources. Collect dew using absorbent rags. Melt snow or ice. Suck on the eyeballs of fish or mammals. With some training you can also learn to build a solar or vegetation still, extract water from local plants, or process water from your urine (Do not drink urine directly; too much salt content and toxins to make it worth the effort).

Discussion:

1. If the spirit of God is boundless and we are provided unlimited access to it, then why might we feel the need at times to ration our spiritual energy?
2. In what ways are the advantages of running water similar to the advantages of a moving spirit?

3. Sucking on eyeballs and distilling urine are des-
    perate measures performed by those desperate
    for hydration. Have you ever performed a "dras-
    tic" spiritual act to obtain living water?

Scripture for Reflection:

1. Mark 9:41. By the grace of Christ we can
    become a source of living water.
2. John 7:37-39. The real fountain of youth.

Disinfection: The goal of disinfection is to kill (steri-
lize) any dangerous life forms that might exist in water
and remove them from our drink. There are a host of
nasty life forms and byproducts that exist in water supplies, waiting to take advantage of the non-discrimi-
nate consumer: bacteria, viruses, protozoa and worms.
They are supremely adapted for survival, lying dormant
in near-freezing waters, traveling by way of feces, utilizing multiple host species, and perhaps thriving in
humans for weeks before obvious symptoms occur; and
Lord, what symptoms occur! It can be something as
"subtle" as the runs, headaches or nausea, and progress
into severe diarrhea, cramping and fevers. Water-borne
illness is one of the primary killers of children on the
planet. The blessing, and tragedy, is that prevention is
incredibly easy and effective.

Heat: Boiling water kills the nasties. There is some
controversy as to how long to boil water, especially
since the boiling point of water is in part determined
by altitude above sea level, but most sources agree that

water that reaches the boiling point for a handful of minutes effectively destroys waterborne pathogens. A caveat: Will heat neutralize poisons or toxins? Don't count on it.

You want to get rid of satanic pathogens in your life? Turn up the heat! Not just a little, this can actually result in the multiplication of troubles. Boil it! Even the most hardened cysts will lose their protective shells and explode in the process.

Discussion:

1. What are the spiritual nasties that commonly invade your body?
2. What would it look like in your life to crank up the heat to the boiling point as a means of disinfection?

Chemical: Halogens are chemicals, notably chlorine and iodine, which disinfect water. Effective against most bacteria and viruses, chemicals are readily available in the form of iodine or chlorine tablets. There are limitations to chemical disinfection that the survivor must be aware of, however. Effectiveness is not universal (Cryptosporidium cysts, for example, prove highly resistant). pH, temperature, sediment and time all influence the effectiveness of chemical means. And finally, chemicals can leave your disinfected water with a disagreeable taste that cannot be neutralized until after the disinfecting process has been completed.

Discussion:

1. Think of chemical disinfecting as being the "man-made" way of making your spiritual water safer. This might include self-help groups/authors, psychiatry, and pharmacological means (prescribed drugs). Are such disinfectants effective? Are you currently using such a chemical disinfectant in your life? Are you attuned to its limitations and side effects?

Filtration: All too frequently, there is dangerous sediment, both living and nonliving, floating about within the water that we need to survive. It must be removed. This can be done by sending water through some form of filtration device. There are excellent man-made filters that can be bought specifically for this purpose. Of course, you must have the foresight to have one available prior to the crisis, and you must know how to maintain your filter. In the wild, simple filtration systems can be created by siphoning water through a bandana, allowing water to filter through progressively finer layers of pebbles, sand and charcoal, or simply allowing water to remain still in a container, allowing gravity to force sediment to the bottom. These techniques will not remove most parasites or cysts that may make you ill, but they will remove visible dangers and help eliminate offensive odors, colors and tastes.

Discussion:

1. What are the filtration systems you have in place right now, systems that prevent the visible and obvious trash from infecting your spiritual life?
2. Filters become clogged, rendering them more and more ineffective. How do you maintain your filtration systems? Is there another layer you might add to increase your system's effectiveness?
3. Filtration creates water that is more pleasing to our senses, yet may still be deadly. Like any predator, Satan knows that an attractive lure, innocuous and pleasing to the senses, is the best bait. What seemingly pure influences might pass through your filtration system, yet still contain deadly cysts and viruses?

Scripture for Reflection:

1. 2Kings 2:19-22. Water is healed to benefit a community
2. Psalm 51:2. The ultimate cleansing effect.

X

HOME SWEET HOME: LESSONS FROM SHELTER

I long to dwell in your tent forever and take refuge in the shelter of your wings.

Psalm 61:4

The human body is at once both incredibly resilient and incredibly fragile. God has blessed us with a degree of intellect and a spirit of adaptability that has allowed us to inhabit virtually every ecosphere on the planet. Man can be found thriving in bitter arctic cold, scorching desert heat, tropical islands, boreal forests, savannahs, steppes, and every place in between. At the same time, we have been denied the fur, fat and bio-thermal adaptations necessary to survive without clothing and shelter even under near- ideal conditions, and any man that expects to emerge from a survival crisis must never forget this dichotomy. It is no theological mystery why God's first post-Eden gift to people was a set of new clothes: how long would they have lasted without such shelter?

Shelter from rain and wind

It is the classic survival scenario: You are all alone in the wilderness. Night is falling and the sound of strange animals fills the air. With nothing but the ragged clothes on your back, a chill wind begins to blow, and the first frigid drops of icy rain begin to fall. As you turn up your collar and huddle beneath your rapidly dampening jacket you realize that the situation has just changed. It is no longer an uncomfortable night in the woods; it is now a matter of life or death.

Your body is well-adapted to creating a micro-climate immediately around itself. When we are cold, we shiver to generate heat, utilize goose bumps that cause our hair to stand on end and thus trap a layer of warm air next to our skin, restrict blood flow to non-vital body parts, and perform a myriad of other biochemical functions to conserve and generate heat. Unfortunately, all this hard work can be lost the instant that a cool breeze flows across our body. All the energy our body has used to warm up that layer of air immediately surrounding our body is wasted as the wind whisks away the warm air and replaces it with new, cool air. This process, known as convection or wind chill, can rapidly cool a survivor's body to lethal temperatures. Add to that a layer of moisture, be it perspiration, rain, or even condensation, and you are now in serious danger of encountering that wilderness killer: hypothermia.

Your best bet is to ensure that your survival kit contains wind-proof, water-resistant material. An extra large garbage bag is ideal. It is lightweight, wind and water proof, easily packed, and is versatile enough to protect both body and gear. Get one of the orange Halloween versions and you also have a useful signaling device. Space blankets, rain ponchos or windproof clothing make an excellent first line of defense and should be carried with you on even the sunniest of days. And of course, never forget the usefulness of duct tape, both for repairing materials and creating windproof barriers (the army refers to duct tape as "one-hundred-mile-an-hour tape"). I like to keep some wrapped around my water bottle for easy access. Remember that shelter from wind might include a moist handkerchief to protect your mouth and nose or an improvised set of birch bark goggles to protect against stinging sand or snow.

Natural wind and water barriers are much harder to come by. Your best bet is probably using layers of material to create a shingle effect: top layers overlapping bottom ones. Bark, large leaves, branches, and even rocks can be used for this purpose. Frames can be constructed from branches and vines to support your shingle walls (the steeper sloped roof, the better). Moss, mud, snow and grass tufts can all be used to chink shelter walls to inhibit wind effects. Windproof walls can also be made through snow trenches, rock outcroppings or low areas. You must be aware, however, that such formations can become natural wind funnels or gathering points for moisture, thus defeating your objective of maintaining warmth.

In addition to creating shelter that protects you from the temperature effects of wind, you also must bear in mind the hazards of powerful wind. Be aware of widow makers, dead limbs and trees that might come crashing down upon you in a windstorm, firestorms that might race through your area, shelter roofs and walls that might collapse under high winds, snow shelters that might rapidly dissolve under a warm Chinook wind, or blinding sand and dust conditions created by unfavorable winds. Sudden bursts of water can kill too, in the form of flash floods. When building your shelter, especially in a low lying area or natural water channel, be wary of signs indicating prior flooding in the area. A cloudburst miles away can result in a sudden torrent of water that can rush upon the unexpected with amazing force.

And of course, keep in mind the benefits of channeling wind: as an aid to fire-starting, as a means for keeping your campsite free of biting insects, as a cooling agent, and perhaps even generating wind-powered signaling devices.

Discussion:

1. Wind can be a beneficial, productive and cleansing agent in small quantities, yet become a life-threatening, destructive force when unrestrained. What other aspects of your life have this capacity for good or evil, depending upon their restraint?

2. Wind and water penetrate the smallest of cracks and enters at will. Are there cracks in your spir-

itual armor or defenses? How might you chink such cracks?

Scripture for Reflection:

1. Isaiah 25:4. Praise for sure shelter.

Shelter from temperature extremes: Even without wind or precipitation, air temperature can challenge the hardiest survivor. Being the warm-blooded creatures that we are, we must ensure a constant core temperature to conserve energy, maintain health and even perform tasks as simple as eating or sleeping. If our shelter cannot maintain a tolerant air temperature, it is only a matter of time before the negative effects of exposure overwhelm our survival efforts.

Remember that hot air rises, cold air sinks. If you want to stay cool, create a shelter with a high roof and sleep low. If you need more warmth, create a shelter with a low area designed to trap cold air, and sleep higher up. If you have a fire in your shelter, or even a candle, you will feel a noticeable difference in temperature by sleeping higher up. Just remember to provide adequate air flow to prevent the dangers of carbon monoxide poisoning, which will kill you just as quickly and insidiously as exposure will.

Consider building a reflective wall of rock, wood or metal that will transmit heat from your fire back toward you. A space blanket works particularly well for this purpose. Just be aware that a metallic blanket may prove hazardous in an electrical storm...

Lofty materials will trap a layer of air which can then serve as a powerful means of insulation. Do not lay on scorching sand, moist ground or snow, rather, lay down a layer of lofty branches, feathers, or leaves; anything that can be fluffed up to trap air. Remember: thicker and fluffier is better, do not settle for a few inches of material that will rapidly compress as you lay upon it through the night, shoot for two feet or more.

A warning: Remember the story of the frog thrown in a pot of water that slowly began to heat? The frog, unaware of impending danger, swam contently even as it slowly died from the rising temperature. Sometimes the danger comes from the mundane, say an air temperature of fifty degrees with a slight breeze or a humid day at eighty-five degrees. Particularly under the stressors present in a survival situation, these relatively "mild" temperatures can prove insidious, slowly sapping the life from the unwary.

Discussion:

1. Temperature extremes cause the body to become numb and shut down; we simply lose the ability to regulate and self-monitor. What issues in society have you slowly become numb to? How can we regulate and self-monitor to prevent ourselves from suffering the fate of the frog?

2. Some people adapt to heat better, others to cold. Everyone has a comfort zone. When it comes to praising God, where is your comfort zone? Are you comfortable with bold, outward expres-

sions of worship (speaking in tongues, loud praise music, clapping of hands and dancing)? How about deep, internal reflection (meditative prayer, chanting, long moments of silence)? Are you willing or do you ever feel called to step outside of your comfort zone?

Scripture for Reflection:

1. Jonah 4: 5-11. Sometimes learning requires discomfort.

Shelter through clothing: When it comes right down to it, clothing is about protection. Think back to Genesis when God graciously provides Adam and Eve with skin garments, clothing to protect us from the thorns and thistles from a cursed ground, and clothing to protect us from our own shame. Later, we are told to clothe ourselves in splendor, strength, compassion, battle armor and even in the Lord Jesus Christ…clearly there is something to be said for clothing ourselves properly! We want to take care of our garments because they are a gift from God (and let's face it: sack cloth and ashes is *so* last year!). Whether you are sporting sewn animal skins or wearing the latest high tech super fiber, the rules for taking care of your threads are the same: Think COLD (clean, overheating, loose /layered, dry).

Keep clothing clean. Fibers matted down by grease, oil and dirt lose their loft, and when that happens they can no longer trap and warm that essential layer of air that serves as insulation. When at all possible, keep clothing clean. For example, you might wash your socks in a stream or scrub off filth with sand.

Avoid overheating. When performing strenuous survival skills like digging a snow shelter or breaking up firewood it can easily result in overheating: you start to sweat. This is a common mistake and could very well prove a deadly one, because the now-damp clothes will rob your body of valuable heat at a horrific pace. Even once your shelter is done or your fire is constructed, you will still have taken a major step backward by getting your clothing damp. You must avoid overheating.

Dress loose and in layers. As we were fond of saying in Alaska: There is no fashion in the arctic. Your primary concern is trapping that layer of air next to your skin, just like a furbearing animal or a diver in a drysuit. The way to do this is by dressing in layers. Furthermore, this allows you to strip off layers to avoid overheating or add layers when you are sedentary. Why loose? Because it is the circulation of warm blood that keeps your body warm. Restrict the circulation, you restrict the warmth. And while we're on the subject, avoid caffeine, dehydration, alcohol and tobacco, all of which constrict blood vessels and circulation. Loose and layered is the only style to sport when it comes to survival.

Keep dry. Nothing strips a fiber's capability to keep you warm faster than moisture. Cotton, including denim, is notorious for becoming ice cold when wet. Down, one of nature's best insulators, is useless if it gets wet. Even material like wool, which maintains much of its heat retention when wet, is clammy and cold when wet. If at all possible, keep your clothing dry.

This is especially critical for socks and footwear: wet feet translates into soft skin, which very rapidly evolves into blisters, sore spots, and even trench foot. If your feet do become immersed, weigh the pros and cons of starting a fire to dry them out.

Body heat escapes most rapidly where blood vessels are close to the surface. This means that if you want to heat up or cool down more efficiently you should pay particular attention when clothing the head, neck, sides, and groin. Extremities like hands, nose, ears, and feet will give you early warnings about your core temperature and the need for adjusting. Do not ignore these warnings; adjust your levels of clothing at the first signs of discomfort.

Discussion:

1. The Bible at various points says to clothe yourself in splendor, strength, compassion, humility and the Lord Jesus Christ. But what does this mean? How do we do this? And how do we take care of our spiritual garments?

2. As Christians, what message do we want our clothing to communicate to others? Is it vanity to dress in fine clothes? Is it okay to do so if our intent is to dominate a business meeting or attract the attention of a potential mate?

Scripture for Reflection:

1. Genesis 3:21. Even in our sin God blesses us with His divine protection.
2. Ephesians 6:11-17. From animal skins to battle armor, help from the Lord is tailor-made to suit us.

Shelter sites: Selection of a shelter site is critical in a survival situation. By following a few basic principles, using common sense, and practicing shelter construction techniques before actually needing them, the survivalist can find relative comfort under even the most adverse of conditions.

- Avoid damaging wildlife when practicing shelter construction.
- If constructing a permanent site, situate near potable water, firewood source, game trails, and edible plants.
- Consider elevated positions to avoid insect swarms, flood and avalanche hazards and increase visibility for signaling.
- If using a cave, be wary of animal hazards (including bat guano!), sheering rocks, carbon monoxide accumulation and lightning strikes (around entranceways).
- Inspect sleeping area for rocks, ants, wasps, poisonous plants, levelness of ground, signs of water seepage, overhanging branches, solitary trees (lightning hazard), potential rockslide/

avalanche hazard, or anything else that might create a hazardous situation.

- Ensure you can make your way back to your shelter if caught out after nightfall/in fog/in blowing snow.
- Observe camp discipline at all times, including proper latrine construction, food storage, firewood collection, lofting/airing of bedding material, etc.

Discussion:

1. To build our house on solid ground is to build our lives upon Christ. What does this mean in practical terms? Give a solid, real-life example of how you can do this.
2. How is selecting an appropriate shelter site similar to selecting an appropriate church community? What are the results of a wise choice? A poor choice?

Scripture for Reflection:

1. Matthew 7:26-27. A foolish shelter site leads to destruction.
2. Psalm 91:1. Above all else, shelter allows us rest.

XI

LESSONS FROM SUSTENANCE

> John's clothes were made of camel's hair, and
> he had a leather belt around his waist. His food
> was locusts and wild honey.
>
> Matthew 3:4

Yes, you can probably survive without eating for over
a month. Yes, water, shelter and fire are generally considered more pressing concerns in a survival scenario.
But let's face it, when we think of the true survivor we
picture a guy coming back to camp with a grin on his
face and something to put in a cook pot slung over his
shoulder. The true survivor is in it for the long run, and
this means the skills and knowledge necessary to bring
home the bacon (or grubs or berries, or whatever).

Plants: The best way to identify edible plants is to
have a local expert standing next to you (not likely). The
next best way is to have studied the local flora prior to
getting lost and having an illustrated guide book at the
ready (helpful, but not foolproof). Everyone should be
able to identify at least a few common edibles in their
region and know something about their nutritional/
medicinal value. The larger problem then becomes

availability. Just because you can identify blackberries, wood sorrel and Queen Anne's Lace is no guarantee that you will be able to find such delectables in a crisis. There may come a point when you have to take a chance on an unknown plant; the key is doing this without poisoning yourself in the process.

One method of doing this is using what's called the edibility test. It is not foolproof, but it is a reasonable approach to testing unknown plants for edibility in an emergency. It consists of a series of incremental steps designed to detect non-edibility at the earliest stage possible. The edibility tests are deliberately time-consuming, giving your body a chance to decide whether it will tolerate the strange new plant. A typical edibility test would look like this. Rub a portion of the plant on the inner part of your wrist; wait for an hour to see if there is any sort of allergic reaction. Touch a portion of the plant to your lip; again, wait for any adverse reactions like burning, tingling or swelling. Touch a portion of the plant to your tongue; wait and observe. Chew a small piece of the plant and spit it out; wait and observe. Chew a small piece and swallow. Wait eight hours. If you feel nauseas, induce vomiting and drink large quantities of water; if not, continue the test. Chew and swallow a larger piece. Wait eight hours. If there are no adverse effects, it is likely that the plant is safe; not definitely, but likely. Do not try this test with mushrooms; there are too many deadly varieties out there to take the chance.

Discussion:

1. Think of the edibility test. What in your life have you experienced very slowly and cautiously, all the while being wary of possible signs of poison? For example, joining a new social group, exploring a new career, pursuing a romantic relationship, fellowshipping at a new church, etc.

2. Our body generally provides us with warning signs and symptoms of poison. What are the signs and symptoms of spiritual poison? Is there a time in your life when you were being spiritually poisoned without any apparent warning? Did you turn to an expert (Holy Spirit) or consult a guide book (Bible)?

Scripture for Reflection:

1. Genesis 1:29. An abundance beyond comprehension.
2. 1Thessalonians 5:21-22. We are not called to take everything in blindly.

Finger Food: I guess the nice thing about bugs, grubs and critters is that there are so many of them. Many contain significant nutritional value, can be eaten raw, and are relatively easy to catch. Of course, one must get over the squeamishness of consuming such tidbits; easier said than done for many of us, but truthfully, you have probably eaten quite a few insects in your lifetime already without your even knowing it. Most are edible, so let's discuss the exceptions first:

- avoid insects that feed on dung, carrion, or rot: they likely carry infection.
- avoid insects that are slow, brightly colored or bad smelling; they are likely poisonous.
- remove spiny legs, stingers, venom sacs, wings, hairy skin, body armor and heads.
- cook ants for at least six minutes to neutralize formic acid.
- cook, clean and remove body wastes as much as possible.
- snails and slugs can be poisonous; avoid those with bright shells, and starve them for several days on safe greens so that any potential toxins will be excreted. Wash and boil.

Ants and termites are great because they tend to mass together in large quantities. Remove any wings or stingers. They can be mashed into a nutritious paste, boiled, broiled or roasted on hot rocks. Don't forget about the eggs, which can be eaten raw. Grasshoppers have the taste of shrimp (remove hazardous parts first). Bees are edible at all stages of development and have the added benefit of providing honey. Smoking a hive must be done with caution, but the benefits to a hungry survivor can be huge. Aquatic bugs can be eaten, but boil them first to prevent disease from foul water. Snails, worms and slugs are great sources of protein, but should be starved and boiled first to remove potential toxins. Frogs, salamander and newts are all edible, but remove potentially poisonous skin before cooking (frog legs do taste like chicken!). Remember, a snake is a steak. Snakes are great if you can safely kill one, but please, use common sense.

Discussion:

1. In nature, poisonous creatures are often easily identifiable by their brilliance to the eye. Are sinful practices brilliant to the eye? Why are we so attracted to poison when it is clearly labeled as such?

2. Sometimes it is necessary to consume squeamish little tidbits to get us through hard times. What spiritual tidbits have you had to swallow, despite the apprehensive pit in your stomach? Examples: criticism, self-examination, swallowing your pride, committing to a new habit, etc.

Scripture for Reflection:

1. Genesis 3:6. Attractive to the senses does not always equate to something beneficial.
2. Leviticus 11:22. Still the appetizers of choice for many parts of the world.

Fish: The good news: all freshwater fish are edible, many being a valuable source of protein, nutrients and water. In a survival situation, fish can be caught by angling, fish traps, spearing, netting, drugging, tickling, and yes, even using explosives (liberates oxygen in the water). The bad news: anyone who has ever fished before knows that it is not as easy or reliable as you might like. Be creative with your bait, remembering to save any excess innards, insect eggs, etc. that you might have collected previously. Don't forget about ice fishing or night fishing.

Discussion:

1. Jesus calls us to be fishers of men. So, what can we use for bait?
2. There are many ways to catch a fish. What techniques for sharing the message of Christ are you currently employing?

Scripture for Reflection:

1. Leviticus 11:9. Bounty from the deep.
2. Mark 1:7. A different bounty.

Birds: The good news: all birds are edible, although they ought to be thoroughly boiled to destroy parasites, especially in birds of prey or carrion eaters. The bad news: catching a bird is not easy under the best of circumstances. You might try a throwing stick, net, noose or baited trap. I have heard that even a primitive model of an owl will cause other birds to mob it. Look for dropping and tracks that might indicate a nightly roost. And of course, be mindful of finding eggs.

Discussion:

1. In Scripture, birds are often portrayed as scavengers, nuisances and thieves of precious seed. In your life, what scavengers consume your resources of time, energy, patience, etc.?

Scripture for Reflection:

1. Matthew 10:29-31. Worth beyond measure.
2. Matthew 14:4. Beware of he that would snatch away the message.

Small game: Your best bet for securing small game is to acquaint yourself with their habits and signs ahead of time. Stripped bark, remains of nuts, tracks, stripped shoots and droppings are all positive indications of small game. Remember that most animals will not feed in daylight, so hunt accordingly. Acquaint yourself how to make and use several types of traps and snares that can be built under survival conditions. In general, the more traps the better, set at a reasonable distance so as not to waste energy traveling to and fro. Bear in mind that you will have to sacrifice some of your hard-gotten food in order to bait traps. Remember also that even a small snared animal can injure you or attract potentially dangerous scavengers; use caution. Small game is relatively easy to skin and cook, and in general the whole animal (minus bowels and excrement) can be consumed.

Discussion:

1. Catching food sometimes requires giving up food for bait. What small things do you give up with the hope of catching something better?
2. Cite a specific example in your life when something small turned out to be a big blessing.

Big game: Every survivalist's dream: being able to bring down a large game animal. Keep dreaming. The odds of killing big game in a survival situation are slim to none. Reflect carefully on whether or not the time and expended energy are worthwhile. Traps are likely your best bet; just remember that a trap designed to capture and kill a large animal is also capable of maiming or killing a man. Even in a survival situation, mark your traps in a manner that will warn fellow homo sapiens of the danger. If you are fortunate enough to bring down an animal, be aware of predators or scavengers that might also be interested in the kill. Boiling game is the safest way to prevent disease. Avoid animals that behave sickly, and remember to clean your hands before and after preparing game. Try to keep the blood for consumption; it is high in vitamins, salt and minerals. Use the entrails for fishing or bait to attract other animals. It is worth learning how to flesh an animal hide for blankets or clothing. Learn how to preserve meat by drying, smoking and soaking in salt water.

Discussion:

1. Catching big game may mean big risks for big rewards. Hunting takes large amounts of time, sacrificing resources and sometimes even a degree of personal danger. Have you ever gone hunting in a spiritual sense? Taken a big risk for God or for spiritual growth? Planning any hunting expeditions in the foreseeable future?

Scripture for Reflection:

1. Jeremiah 48:44. Remember the hunter can quickly become the hunted.

XII

LIFE AND LIMB: LESSONS FROM FIRST AID

Heal me, O Lord, and I will be healed; save me
and I will be saved, for you are the one I praise.

Jeremiah 17:14

Note Well: *What follows is not a comprehensive first aid
course, it is merely a reflection on commonly practiced pro-
cedures. It is highly encouraged that everyone take the time
to participate in a properly conducted first aid course on a
regular basis. "The life you save could be your own."*

To this point, some readers may still question the
necessity of survival training. After all, the odds of crash
landing in the Amazon, breaking down in the desert or
being stranded in the middle of the Pacific are pretty
miniscule. And with the advent of GPS, satellites and
cell phones and plain old urban sprawl it would seem
we are never far from help.

All true, but here is another way to look at it: injury
or illness changes everything. A dead branch falling on
your head, a twisted ankle, even something as small as

a sliver under your fingernail can totally ramp up the urgency of a situation. Even the most prudent survivalist is subject to injury or illness and the change in mindset that follows, and from a spiritual perspective here is the reality: we will all be wounded, we are all in need of healing.

The principles of survival previously discussed (Part I) coincide perfectly with the preliminary steps to providing first aid: You must first recognize that an emergency exists (Acknowledge the Crisis), overcome emotional barriers and decide to act (Choose Life), contact 9-1-1 (Send out a Distress Signal), secure the scene and perform triage (Assess the Environment), and decide whether to move the patient (Decision to Move). Let's continue the analogy and talk about providing care.

Scene Survey: Take in the situation in its entirety. Do not be so fixated on one person or wound that you ignore the big picture (this happened to me once in a training situation: I was so intent on treating a broken arm that I failed to notice the guy had been shot through the abdomen). Above all, ensure that the scene is safe. Running into traffic, a room filled with smoke, or a crime scene can rapidly transform you from being rescuer number one to victim number two. See if you can determine the cause of injury. Look around for other people who may be able to tell you what happened, give you information on the patients, or provide assistance. It seems like a lot, but most of these steps can be accomplished in a matter of seconds, even as you are approaching the scene. And don't forget to take a calming deep breath. This applies whether you are a rescuer or the actual patient.

Discussion:

1. What are some steps you can take when providing spiritual counseling to make the scene safer?
2. Why is taking a deep breath so important? Can you do this spiritually?

Scripture for Reflection:

1. Mark 13:33. We must always be taking in the situation.
2. Ephesians 6:18. Alert, always seeking help.

Activate the EMS: This is just a fancy way of saying call 9-1-1 or get professional help. If in a crowd, don't just say, "Someone call for help!" Someone too often translates into Noone. When calling, be ready to give a location, the number of patients involved, and a rough idea of their condition (Are they breathing? Have a pulse? Conscious?). Many times you can have someone else calling while you are doing an initial check of the patient. People often wonder if the injury is extreme enough to call in the professionals; I would say this: if you have any doubt, give the pros a shout. 9-1-1 operators are trained to help you assess emergency situations. And never hang up until the operator tells you to.

Discussion:

1. How does calling 9-1-1 relate to prayer?
2. If God is the 9-1-1 operator in your life, who are His paramedics?

Scripture for Reflection:

1. Psalm 5:2. Never hesitate to activate the EMS.
2. Psalm 106:4. As true now as it was back then.

ABCs: There are some situations where seconds count. Your body craves oxygen so much that cells, including brain cells, will begin to die in a handful of minutes. You *must* ensure the patient has an open Airway, is Breathing, and has blood Circulating (ABC). The steps to doing this are simple and can be learned in most first aid courses, yet some people are hesitant to act. It could be fear of disease or a lawsuit. It could be fear of doing the wrong thing and making things worse. Sometimes it is the panic of knowing the patient personally. Or perhaps it is the hope that someone else will step in. Whatever the case, it is often helpful to make a commitment to act and receive training before it becomes necessary.

Discussion:

1. What are the absolutely critical, time-essential, die-without steps you need to take to ensure your spiritual life will not be lost?

2. What are the obstacles that prevent you from ensuring others are receiving this level of emergency care?

Scripture for Reflection:

1. Genesis 2:7. The importance of breath, mind-boggling in its simplicity.
2. 1Chronicles 22:19. The true importance of the heart.

Stop the bleeding: Every culture in every time period has recognized the relationship between blood and life. A person who loses too much blood will die just as assuredly and for the same reason that a flame will die without oxygen. You must stop severe bleeding, and you must do so quickly. The simplest technique is to apply direct pressure to the wound. If the patient can do this, great, if not, it is recommended that you use some type of waterproof barrier to prevent transmission of disease. The easiest way is to keep a pair of first-aid gloves readily available, but a piece of plastic, a Gortex jacket, a shower curtain, or any sort of waterproof barrier can be used in a pinch.

If there is no danger of exacerbating a broken bone or producing further injury, the patient should be positioned so that the source of bleeding is higher than the heart. This could mean elevating an arm, having the person lie down, etc. Once pressure has been applied, do not remove it, this can cause the bleeding to begin anew with even greater force. Learn how to apply a pressure bandage and always have one handy in your travels. In a pinch you can use a feminine hygiene pad, a clean cloth or another body part. And remember, stopping life-threatening bleeding quickly is a higher priority than finding a sterile dressing. The use of tourniquets is problematic, requires advanced training, and is rarely necessary. Direct pressure and elevation will staunch most severe bleeding situations and is easy to learn.

Discussion:

1. Have you experienced a time when you felt like your life-giving energy was being drained away? How can you stop such bleeding?
2. If you are treating someone else who is spiritually "bleeding," what protective measures should you take to prevent "disease transmission?"

Scripture for Reflection:

1. Luke 8:44. Bleeding stopped through elevation.
2. Matthew 26-27-28. The awesome power of blood.

Treat for Shock: A simple definition of shock is a disruption of the circulatory system and its job in delivering oxygen-rich blood throughout the body. The heart, blood and blood vessels must all be sound in order for this to happen. It must be treated. Expect shock to occur during any accident and be prepared to treat for it. The treatment is simple: have the person lie down to reduce pain and increase comfort; control bleeding, maintain a normal body temperature, loosen any clothing or jewelry that might be restricting circulation and provide reassurance. All these steps will help the blood flow more readily through a stressed circulatory system. What might not be obvious is this: do not allow a person to eat or drink, even water. Not only will this divert blood to unnecessary digestive organs, it will also increase the odds that a person will vomit, a major concern if the person needs to have surgery. Continue to monitor the patient and call for help. If left untreated, shock kills.

Discussion:

1. Persons who undergo a tragedy such as the death of a loved one are said to be in a state of shock. It can be very difficult to know how to aid someone in such a condition. What are some possible treatment steps?

2. Shock manifests itself differently in different people. It can be especially difficult to detect in the very old or the very young. Who in your life should you be extra vigilant toward? Is it possible to recognize and treat emotional shock in yourself?

Scripture for Reflection:

1. Isaiah 40-31. Shock treatment.

Checking a Patient: At this point you should conduct a head-to-toe evaluation of your patient. Head to toe helps prevent you from missing something and if the patient is conscious, this is a good opportunity to establish rapport, gather information and provide comforting. Even if the person is unconscious, I like to talk aloud: it helps my confidence, reduces the chances of skipping steps, and allows bystanders to know what's going on.

In a nutshell, checking a patient means using all your senses to determine if something is out of the ordinary. One pupil big, the other small? Labored breathing? Some sort of medical ID bracelet? A hard lump in the abdomen? These all could be useful in determining the next course of action. Even if you lack the training necessary to treat an injury or illness, it is still useful to interview a conscious patient. First, this provides psychological first aid. Speak in a comforting and reassuring manner. This does not mean lying: telling a patient whose leg is half ripped off that, "Everything is okay" will not instill trust in your medical competence. Far better to say, "You've had an accident, but I have called for help and I won't leave you." Second, if the person does go unconscious, you may have gained some valuable information that you can share with paramedics when they do arrive: How old is the patient? Any known allergies or medications? Pregnant? Someone I can contact?

Discussion:

1. There is often great comfort in the presence of another during a difficult time. Do you sense the presence of God in your times of trial? Do you truly believe He is present, competent and caring? If not, why?

2. Patients may have signs and/or symptoms. A sign is something that another person can detect (irregular breathing, skin discoloration, bleeding). Who in your life helps you detect abnormalities in your spirit? A symptom is something that you feel but might not be detected by others (nausea, dizziness, headache). How often do you inventory your spirit (an "examination of conscience") to see if any abnormalities exist?

Scripture for Reflection:

1. 1Corinthians 11:28. A life-saving evaluation.

PART III:

ANALOGIES FROM ENVIRONMENT

When we speak of a biome, we are speaking of a region with a specific climate, vegetation and animal life; in short, we are describing *circumstances*. Circumstances will change throughout life, offering scenarios as radically different as the desert and the jungle, the mountains and the city. But regardless of the "biome" we find ourselves currently in, there is a lesson to be found. A consummate survivor will actively seek the lesson, learn from it, and add this wisdom to the survival kit. The scripture passages that accompany these readings are not designed to directly correlate with the text, but are merely designed to help you think thematically about the topic at hand. As you read the analogies that follow, pause often and reflect upon how you interact in various situations, and never forget Saint Paul's admonitions: to be content and give thanks in all circumstances (Philippians 4:11, Thessalonians 5:18).

XIII

ANALOGY OF THE DESERT: MODERATION

Like a city whose walls are broken down is a
man who lacks self-control.

Proverbs 25:28

We have a problem with moderation. In the secular
world we see this manifested through budget deficits,
eating disorders, alcoholism, gambling, workaholics,
addictions, obsessions, etc. In the spiritual realm we
come across the sins of gluttony, sloth, jealousy, lust,
and so on. And though our society pays great lip service to these problems, "How much is enough?" seems
to be a dilemma we are unable to resolve. But for the
desert nomad, this lesson can break down into two
simple rules: avoid too much sun and too little water;
and those who ignore or violate these commandments
will quickly discover just how frail the human condition is…

Some would say that human physiology is wonderfully designed to endure the rigors of the sun. The body

types and limbs of desert dwellers tend to be long and
lean; perfect for dissipating heat through high surface
area. There is little fat storage, as fat serves to insu-
late and retain heat. Pupils contract to reduce excessive sunlight. Blood circulation allows the heat from
deep within the body to proceed to the surface where it
can be released through the skin. The process of sweat
evaporation further allows our bodies to remove excess
heat. Skin color darkens to block dangerous ultraviolet
radiation. And our brain constantly monitors internal
conditions, actively transferring excessive heat away
from critical areas to high-need organs, while all the
while regulating metabolism.

Sounds great, right? Don't kid yourself. In the desert
day-time temperatures can exceed 120 degrees, heating
the sand below to over 150 degrees. Our bodies, incapable of withstanding an internal temperature increase
of even ten degrees, will short-circuit in a handful of
days. But first, stomach cramps develop as the brain
diverts blood flow to critical areas. Blood thickens to
the point that it can no longer flow out of the gashes
that develop as skin succumbs to first, second and
third-degree burns. Delicately folded protein mol-
ecules begin to unfold. Hallucinations and outer body
experiences begin as higher brain functions shut down.
Metabolic functions, which accelerate uncontrollably
with temperature, rocket to unsustainable levels until
even the most protected portions of the brain experience irreversible chemical pandemonium. Compared
to the thermonuclear power of the sun, our biologi-

cal adaptations are a joke. Too much sun kills (2Peter 3:12).

But water is the great panacea. With its ability to flow from high concentration to low, absorb massive amounts of heat, and expend this heat through the process of evaporation, water can drastically offset the detrimental effects of the sun, and our bodies, mostly water to begin with, are superbly designed to conserve water. When concentrations become low our brain produces the message, "I thirst," and we seek to refill. Loss of water through respiration is reduced by histamines that restrict capillaries in the lungs. The pituitary gland instructs the kidneys to reduce water consumption. Blood volume, sodium content and potassium are constantly monitored and regulated to maximize water levels. All within a body encapsulated by skin perfectly designed to be nearly water impermeable. It would seem that these intricate biological adaptations could get us through some really hot spots.

Reality check: given the temperature and humidity levels of the desert, you will die from lack of water in under a week. Every function of your body requires water; just sitting around doing nothing will result in a loss of two liters of water per day. Thirst and dark urine might be your first warning signs. Sweat, fatigue, dizziness and cramping will soon follow. Your heart will have to pump harder as your blood begins to thicken and electrolyte balances will collapse. Your very cells will explode from salt imbalance. As your brain diverts water away from the digestive system, your kidneys and liver will begin to shut down. When you stop sweating and your face becomes dry and pale, you know you have reached the stage of heatstroke; death will visit you in hours. Too little water kills.

Moderation is the lesson from the desert. Too much sun can kill us, but so can too little. Too little water can kill us, but so too can too much (ask anybody who has experienced the rapidity of a flash flood roaring out of a desert canyon). If we cannot learn moderation, we will at best suffer, and at worst perish painfully (2Peter 5-6).

Our bodies can help us learn this message. When functioning properly, our body will tell us when it is time to drink and eat, when it is time to sleep, when it is time to stop and desist. However, many of our problems with moderation arise when we ignore such messages, or through our own misuse, create bodies that prove incapable of sending healthy messages.

Our brains too, aid us in the process. A healthy brain knows best how to allocate resources, monitor the environment, and when necessary, override the demands of the body. But as we have just learned, the body and brain alone stand no chance against the harsh conditions life will immerse us in. As wonderfully designed as humans are, we cannot count on our bodies or our brains to make decisions about moderation (Proverbs 12:15).

Community is our next line of defense. An advocate outside of self, whether this is a caring individual, a faith family, or a national initiative can be just the regulation we need to achieve balance. A community can create a strong and vibrant culture, and such a culture can avail us much in the game of survival. Technology and customs can be introduced that could allow us to survive under conditions that would be quite impossible for the naked individual.

Again, several problems unfold. Think of the alcoholic whose community consists of life-long drinking buddies. Or the customs of a community that find no flaw in the exploitation of women for profit. Or the technology that offers one thousand sites encouraging promiscuity for each one encouraging marital fidelity. And if this isn't enough, community can transform a desert experience into one so comfortable (think "Vegas") that we actually overlook the very lesson we were meant to learn from the desert in the first place: moderation.

Moderation requires balance. However, balance is not giving everything equal weight, it is giving everything appropriate weight. But how do we do this? If our bodies, brains, communities and culture are unreliable, it seems an impossible task. That is why we have been given the ultimate line of defense: spiritual discernment. God gives each of us the ability to find balance, receiving the peace and comfort that comes from living a life according to His will (2Peter 1:5-8). How do we obtain this spiritual discernment? I know of only two ways, the same two ways that Jesus used when He found Himself in a "desert-ed place." The same tactics He used at the onset of His missionary, the same stratagems He developed when confronting the devil while in the desert (Matthew 4). The same skills you must practice and develop in order to understand moderation: fasting and prayer. Pursue these with vigor and spiritual discernment and moderation will be a sure reward.

The powers of our body, the abilities of our brain, technology, community…these are incredible implements for facing the trials of environment. But know this, they will all fall short, they will all malfunction and be out of reach when you need them the most. At some point you will find yourself in the desert, desperately trying to balance the too much and the too little, with your very life in the balance. To welcome this reality, to prepare for this inevitability, this is the lesson of the desert.

Discussion:

1. How would you define moderation?
2. What is the relationship between moderation and delayed gratification? Is Christianity's message one of delayed gratification?
3. Is fasting a form of moderation? What about abstinence? Tithing?
4. Too much or too little kills. Can you think of exceptions to this rule?
5. Where do our fleshly desires come from? Why are we born with appetites that can lead to destruction?
6. Does moderating physical desires (hunger, thirst, breathing, sex) benefit us spiritually?
7. What is the difference between a need and a want? What are the needs of a Christian? The wants?

8. What is the relationship between sacrifice and moderation?
9. Evaluate the following statement: sometimes moderation means not at all.
10. Evaluate the statement: the opposite of moderation is slavery (2Peter2:19).

XIV

ANALOGY OF THE MOUNTAIN: ACCOUNTABILITY

...Everything is uncovered and laid bare before the eyes of him to whom we must give account.

Hebrews 4:13

I work as a teacher for at-risk youth. Put simply, this means that those students who have struggled in the mainstream school environment are relocated to my classroom for a period of time that may last anywhere from an hour to a year. The circumstances that result in a student being placed in my care are many: drug issues, violence, blatant insubordination, poor attendance and criminal activity to name just a few. But the common thread that I see bonding almost every one of my young wards together is this: a lack of accountability. When entering the classroom, the first words I hear from a student almost always run along the theme of, "It's not my fault." To be sure, we could all make strong cases that circumstances beyond our control brought us to places we did not want to be, but at some point in our march toward maturity we need to buck up and admit, "I am responsible for my own actions, my own reactions and my own outlook on life. I hold myself accountable."

When embarking on a wilderness adventure there are few things more crucial than having a partner accountable for his or her own actions. At best, a person without accountability is like a mosquito buzzing in your ear: "Dude, this cheap flashlight keeps screwing up, I can't believe my mom didn't buy me a better one. Mind if I borrow yours again?" At worst, the unaccountable partner jeopardizes the mission and the lives of those involved: "Hey, I thought I knew how to tie that knot! It's not my fault if it keeps slipping out. You should have checked it anyway!"

But even more important, you want a partner who will hold himself accountable for the safety of his partner. There are some places on the planet that you don't want to be caught without someone looking out for your personal well-being, and one place where this is extremely critical is on the side of a mountain.

There are a host of factors that can get you killed when you find yourself treading on an inclined surface somewhere above the snow line, some of which are in your control, many others that are not. Bad weather, rock conditions, equipment failure, injury and lapses in judgment can all lead to your demise. While it is true that meticulous planning, top-notch equipment, experience and sound judgment can all tilt the scales in your favor, I would argue that the greatest asset is climbing with a suitable partner, one who is observant, honest, knowledgeable, and looking out for your best interests (Ecclesiastes 4:10).

Perhaps the greatest symbol of partnership in alpine climbing is this: there is a rope connecting you with your partner. When one falls, both are at risk, both are responsible for arresting the fall. This is generally done by rapidly throwing one's self belly down against the side of the mountain and digging in with an ice axe and boot spikes known as crampons. Your partner is attempting the same maneuver, and on a good day the fall is quickly arrested and the climb can proceed. If conditions are bad or technique sloppy, however, the end result can be both climbers hurtling down the mountain at breakneck speed, sometimes winding up shooting off a cliff face or into a bottomless crevasse, never to be seen again. Being roped to another human being means being ever mindful of keeping the correct tautness; keeping things too tight can yank someone off their feet, keeping things too loose makes stopping a slide much more difficult. When you rope in with a partner, you are accepting both a great risk and a great responsibility; tying the knot with someone is never to be taken lightly (Ecclesiastes 4:12).

Good partners are always aware of one another, both physically and emotionally. This is critical to survival because it is impossible to take a good look at yourself while climbing a mountain. Checking your cheeks for frostbite, monitoring an oxygen valve, looking for twists in a chest harness are tasks made infinitely easier when using the buddy system. But in order to properly monitor your partner there are two knowledge bases that must be in place: 1) you must have accurate information as to what is safe and what is not, and 2) you must know your partner's base-line, in order to determine if something is normal or beginning to go out of synch.

For example, it is pointless to check your partner's harness and knot arrangement if you are unaware of what a proper harness rig should look like. Likewise, you cannot warn of potential avalanche danger if you don't know what avalanche conditions are (Proverbs 13:20). As to the second point, it will be difficult to determine whether your partner is acting strangely if you don't know what normal behavior is. Is your partner singing a quirky off-key yodel because that is what he always does when feeling good, or is this the first signs of oxygen deprivation? Is he cranky because he always gets this way around lunchtime, or is this an early sign of hypothermia? You will only be able to tell if you have knowledge of your partner's baseline.

Honest communication is mandatory with your climbing partner. I would hate for my partner to lie to me about anything, no matter how trivial, because trivial matters snowball into life-and-death consequences on the side of a mountain (Proverbs 18:6-7). If I ask, "How are you feeling?" I am not looking for a generic, "all right." By the same token, if he asks my impression of a tricky bit of moraine, I better not let my ego stand in the way of a straightforward response. And perhaps most difficult, we can never let pride or disappointment or selfish motives prevent us from verbalizing: "I can't make it today. It is time to turn around and return to safety. I hope you will try again with me another day."

Obstacles to communication multiply as circumstances deteriorate. Who wants to talk when the temperature drops to thirty below and every inhale causes you to go into a fit of coughing? Heck, you have been up for thirty hours with an oxygen-deficit headache, your muscles are like rubber, and it feels like you're running a marathon while trying to suck your breath through a drinking straw. You want to climb as deep as you can inside your parka where you can have the luxury of feeling miserable in private. Warning: this is the time where inattentiveness and self-isolation will get you killed. This is the time when you must force yourself to come outside of your own being and monitor the environment, pay attention to what your partner is doing. Communicate or die.

Finally, ensure that you have a partnership where trust is the norm. You may be in a situation where you lose sight of your partner. Whiteouts, snow blindness and plunges into a crevasse can leave you feeling horribly exposed and isolated. Will you trust the partner relationship? You may find yourself incapacitated by circumstances beyond your control as you succumb to Acute Mountain Sickness or frostbite, or hypothermia. Will you have faith and reassurance when your partner says, "I'm going to get us out of here"? This kind of trust doesn't automatically kick in at the start of disaster. It is built, day by day, growing or diminishing through every trial and success. It is a habit. It is a relationship.

Accountability begins with you. It means coming to the base of the mountain with the skills and attitude necessary for you to succeed. You have personally checked all your gear, you have taken it upon yourself to be physically fit and emotionally ready to meet the challenge. You acknowledge any shortcomings and take responsibility for correcting them.

Accountability matures when two people clip into one rope (Proverbs 18:24). It means accepting responsibility not only for yourself but for another. Time and energy have been spent forging a relationship. There is awareness, communication and trust. When everything has been said and done, it is the only one to successfully summit a peak and return to safety.

Discussion:

1. Accountability begins with a standard: this is what I will live up to. As a Christian, what standard do I profess to have? Have I set my standards too high? Too low?

2. Once a standard is set, an accountable person declares: I will take personal responsibility for meeting this standard, no excuses. Do we really believe this? We can all think of examples when circumstances overwhelmed us. As a Christian, is it ever acceptable to say, "It's not my fault"?

3. In alpine survival, an accountability partner must have awareness, honesty and knowledge, all while looking out for their partner's best

interests. What attributes would be crucial for a spiritual accountability partner?

4. There is a certain sense of freedom and adventure one gets when climbing solo. There are no restraints, all your senses are on overdrive, and there is often a huge gain in self-discovery. The risks are obvious. What might it look like to "go solo" spiritually? Given the intensity of the rewards and risks, is it ever acceptable to do this?

5. We speak of an accountability partner, but in Search and Rescue operations, the ideal rope team is often considered to be three people. What are the advantages to a three-man team for spiritual operations? Can you think of any disadvantages?

6. Roping in with another person is an ultra-serious declaration of trust and responsibility. Complete the following sentences:

   In tying the knot with you, I will always…
   I will never…

7. In alpine survival stories you will occasionally come across a story in which a climbing partner must sever his rope to preserve his life or the life of his partner. Once you have tied in with a spiritual partner, is it ever acceptable to cut the rope?

8. There is certainly a subconscious awareness that develops when you work with a partner long enough. You know when something is not right instinctively. But when conditions become extreme, you lose this instinct and you

must depend on a conscious checklist to keep each other safe. What "extreme" life conditions distance you from partner awareness? What conscious safety steps can you take to avoid this distancing?

9. Honest communication is critical with your partner. However, at times pride, jealousy, or simple indifference cause a communication breakdown. At some point you will experience snow blindness or a whiteout. There must be a pre-arranged plan to reestablish communication during a crisis. When have you experienced such a crisis? How do you go about restoring broken lines of communication?

10. Even the most accountable partner makes mistakes, sometimes with catastrophic results. It may be possible to forgive a partner for inattention, poor judgment or lack of knowledge, even though all these things can get you killed. But perhaps there is nothing more heart-wrenching than a partner who abandons you in the wilderness. How does one go about reestablishing a sense of trust when the unthinkable happens, and you are left staring at a cut rope in your hand?

XV

ANALOGY OF THE DEEP: JUST VISITING

Hug the shore; let others try the deep. Primal Life began in the sea. Whether you're the evangelical Christian who takes a literal interpretation of Genesis or the hard-core atheist sporting the Darwin fish on the back of your ride, few would dispute the theory that the origins of life on this planet came forth from the waters. Indeed, water is so connected to life that there is no species on this planet that can function without it. The oceans of today are home to an amazing array of life-forms, both discovered and not, that have adapted an incredible array of biological strategies to survive under the waves. Mankind is not one of those life-forms. Indeed, the depths of the sea rank as one of the most inhospitable places on the planet for human beings. There are some places we were not meant to dwell.

Imagine you were given the task of creating a biome least accommodating to human physiology. You might design an environment where every one of our senses are distorted or rendered useless. Balance, equilibrium and gravity are thrown out the window. The very act of inhalation becomes a death sentence. Individual body cells explode as the body contracts into excruciating spasms of pain and paralysis. Remaining in this environment of torture results in death, yet fleeing results in an equally painful and certain demise. Surrounded by alien life-forms, reality distorts and fades, and your brains retreats into insanity shortly before the very air you have lived with all your life becomes toxic and destroys your every cell. Yet, it would not be necessary to design such an environment, for it already exists. Welcome to life beneath the waves. Welcome to the deep (Genesis 6:17).

Man- a creature primarily composed of water, spending the first nine months of life within a liquid-filled life-support chamber, requiring water every day of our lives spent on a water-logged planet, is not designed to live underwater. Without some form of protection, we would find our submerged bodies unconscious in the time it takes to listen to a Top 40 song on the radio and rapidly approaching death before the end of the next tune.

Yet, such is our attraction to the depths that we have sought for millennia to overcome our natural deficiencies in an effort to dwell beneath the waves, if only for a brief period of time. And through the use of technology and ingenuity, the results have been impressive. Beginning with the simple technique of hyperventilating and trapping air beneath inverted bowls, we have progressed to the degree that a person can spend months travelling underwater without once taking a breath of fresh salt air. Granted, such a feat requires an expenditure of money and technology that is out of reach for most people (and nations), but even the average person can sample a taste of life in the deep through the pursuit of scuba diving.

The key requirement for scuba is implicit in its name: Self Contained Underwater Breathing Apparatus, in other words, an air tank. This device, along with everything else you might possibly need to overcome the body's shortcomings, can be provided by a local dive shop. A suit of neoprene rubber closely hugging your skin will trap a layer of water next to your warm skin, where it remains trapped and warm: a "wetsuit," allowing you to withstand the cooling effects of ocean water flowing across your body. Or, you can go to the next level with a watertight "dry suit," that prevents water from contacting your skin in the first place, allowing you to wear dry insulating layers similar to long underwear. Your naturally buoyant body will have difficulty staying submerged, so a system of weights in the form of a belt will be pre-measured and attached to your waist. And to further assist in the process of ascending and descending, an air bladder will be strapped to your back in the form of a buoyancy control device (BCD). This can be emptied through a purge valve and filled from the air tanks firmly attached to your back. This life-providing air supply makes it into your lungs through a tube that ends in a regulator. Simply bite lightly on the regulator and breathe normally; the pressure sensitive device will ensure a continuous supply of air on demand.

With temperature control, depth control, and an air supply, you will now be able to survive under water. But there are other niceties you will want to have on hand. Since your eyes will be unable to focus light waves as they refract through water, you will need a pair of goggles to provide an airspace for refocusing. And in order to prevent your inner ear from painfully pinching as you descend, your mask conveniently comes with a soft rubber nosepiece, allowing you to pinch the nose shut while breathing firmly with closed lips. This "valsava technique" allows you to equalize air pressure in the ears as you begin your descent.

Flippers will propel you with surprising speed and allow you to maneuver with relative ease. Your arms are best left in a streamlined position close to your body, occasionally being used to manipulate your compass, submersible pressure gauge or BCD. As you continue your descent, the natural spectrum of colors associated with sunlight will begin to fade, and you will want to keep an underwater flashlight handy. A dive knife is essential should you become entangled in seaweed or fishing lines. Cameras, writing slates, marine identification charts and maybe even a spear gun are just some of the optional gear available to help round out your dive. With the proper gear and training, scuba diving is a safe, fascinating recreational pursuit allowing most anyone to experience the thrill of otherworldly adventure (Genesis 1:20-21).

Here's the reciprocal to that equation: it can also get you killed in a variety of horribly painful ways. It could be a failure in any of the aforementioned gear. Regulators fail, valves jam and hoses burst, all of which could leave you without air at depth, which will likely result in a panic reaction leading to an increased heart and respiratory rate, requiring an even greater amount of unavailable oxygen. A cracked faceplate on your swim mask, a broken flipper strap or dead battery in your submersible pressure gauge could quickly spiral into a life-or-death situation.

Or it could be an unexpected happenstance. A curious sea lion severs your regulator line, a current is stronger than you expected and sweeps you toward danger, a piece of unseen coral causes a bleeding gash in shark-infested waters. You try to plan for every contingency, but there is always an unplanned event that can put you in the danger zone in a heartbeat (for me this happened when I began to unexpectedly and violently vomit at a depth of ninety feet below the surface of the Pacific).

It could be the smallest lapse in judgment by you or your dive partner (Matthew 14:28-31). This could be miscalculating how long to allow for an ascent from an undersea wreck, kicking up a blinding cloud of silt while exploring an undersea cave or even surfacing too far from your surface craft. Descending too deep can force nitrogen gas into your brain cells, resulting in a condition not unlike being intoxicated: nitrogen narcosis can produce paranoia, hallucinations and fits of laughter. Ascending too quickly can force nitrogen bubbles to form in your bloodstream, resulting in blockage of blood vessels, loss of vision and hearing, and pain so excruciating that you are forced to curl up into a tight ball: a condition known as "the bends." Coming or going, the very nitrogen that composes 78 percent of every breath you take on the surface can kill you in the deep.

The ocean depths are a vast and enticing world, filled with mystery, adventure and incredible beauty. The lure of the sea has always existed, and now with affordable technology more people than ever can dive into her realm. But we must maintain the mindset of a pilgrim on a sojourn through an inhospitable land. Our man-made protection and judgment can fail us in so many ways, reminding us in a brutal manner that we were not designed to be in such a place for but the briefest of times. There are some places we are not meant to dwell.

Discussion:

1. There is an expression among scuba divers: plan the dive and dive the plan. It means simply that before undertaking a potentially danger-ous event a plan must be put into place and any deviation from the plan increases the likelihood of danger. What type of dive are you planning in your faith? What would it look like to deviate from this plan and what would the results be?
2. God has given us remarkably inquisitive minds, resulting in some pretty fantastic pieces of tech-nology. These tools have allowed us to go places

and do things never before possible, be it in the area of medicine, artificial technology, or undersea exploration. At what point does "using our God-given talents for His glory" turn into "vain men building the tower of Babel?" How do we know when our excitement to discover and design crosses the line?

3. The Bible speaks of having us put on protective gear when entering a hostile environment, like a soldier armoring up before battle (Ephesians 6:18). Does this God-given gear require maintenance on our part? If so, how do we do so?

4. Every sense can deceive us in the water: vision blurs, we cannot determine the direction and distance of a noise, up feels like down, and so on. Feelings sway from moment to moment. Logic crumbles as a nitrogen-drunk brain tries to interpret false data, and we are left with a horribly warped sense of reality. It's easy to say, "Trust God above all things," but how do we do this? How can we really make any decision with confidence that we are in God's will when our flesh is so easily deceived?

5. Scripture says that the earth is the Lord's, and everything in it (Psalm 24:1), that Man has been given dominion and power by God to tend to the earth (Genesis 1:28). Scripture also says that the earth is the domain of the devil, that Jesus is not of this world (John 18:36). So which is it? Is the earth God's beautiful handiwork or Satan's playground?

6. The smallest lapse in judgment can get you or
    your dive partner killed. We must act responsi-
    bly, of course. But how can we do so when we
    are afflicted by environmental forces beyond our
    control? Are we responsible for the life of our
    dive partner when nitrogen literally anesthe-
    sizes our brain? Are circumstances beyond our
    control, such as exhaustion, mental anguish or
    clinical depression a legitimate excuse for sin-
    ful behavior?

7. Analyze these statements:

    We were not created to be long of this world.
    Those who become too comfortable in the
    world are destined to die an anguishing death.

8. We are called to spread the gospel message
    across the entire face of the earth, to all peo-
    ples (Matthew 28:19). Are there some places we
    are not meant to go? More specifically, are there
    places you were not meant to go, even to spread
    the gospel?

XVI

ANALOGY OF THE JUNGLE: TRUST YOUR GUIDE

> ...and the forest claimed more lives that day
> than the sword.
>
> 2Samuel 18:8

The youth of today are somewhat shocked when I relate stories from my childhood. Growing up in the late seventies (yes, 1970s) was radically different from today, as even a cursory glance around my house testifies: no microwave, cable TV (we had 3 channels, black and white), computers, cell phones (we actually *dialed* our black AT&T landline), Velcro, Post-it notes, seatbelts with shoulder straps, dimmer light switches, digital watches/calculators/anything…you get the idea. When we wanted to find out information, we logged onto this thing called a "book." No, not an E-book, just plain old "book." And inside you could manually access all kinds of sources of entertainment and knowledge.

Which was a mixed blessing. As it turned out, there are some things you cannot master from the pages of a book. Like this thing called, "rappelling." The art of rappelling consists of zipping down a fixed rope through a series of bounds made possible by threading the rope through a metal clip called a carabiner. My partner-in-crime and I had likely seen rappelling on one of the hit TV shows at the time (*The A-Team? Dukes of Hazzard?*), and it seemed like the perfect Saturday afternoon activity for bored adolescents. So, after thumbing through a library book, I figured I had sufficiently mastered the basics enough to hurl myself from the upper branches of a large maple tree with my equally knowledgeable buddy standing beside me. The details are rather fuzzy, but I do recollect the sound of screaming, a feeling of free-fall, and my partner reaching out to grab a handful of my stylishly long 1970s hair-do (Shades of Absalom, 2Samuel 18:9).

You can't learn everything from a book (Acts 8:26-31). Or, to update the moral of the story, you can't learn everything from a website, download or video link. And while this holds true everywhere you go, perhaps nowhere else is this point made more clearly than in the jungle.

Jungles contain the richest diversity of life on the face of the planet. In addition to an incredible array of edible plants and animals, there is water aplenty, warm tropical weather, natural medicines, unlimited building materials and navigable river ways; in short everything you need not only to survive, but to live a life of ease. It would seem that any fit individual, dropped in the middle of a jungle with a decent survival manual and a machete could be making out like Robinson Crusoe in no time. Reality check: Odds are you would be dead, or wish you were dead, in the space of a week.

Because while it is true that jungles contain an incredible quantity and variety of life forms, it is also true that each and every species is in competition with one another, and after eons of such competition, jungle flora and fauna have developed an astounding array of defense mechanisms, making it one of the deadliest places on the planet.

Sure, there are thousands of edible plant species. Problem is, they grow right next to plants containing ricin, strychine, and alkaloid solanidine- compounds used to create neurotoxins and biological weapons of mass destruction. Eat one of these and the results can be anything from vomiting and diareah to hallucinations, blindness, seizures, paralysis and death. Are you really confident you can study a guidebook to edible plants and steer clear of danger?

But you don't even have to consume jungle flora to get in trouble. There are plants with syringe-like leaves that will inject venom into whoever is unfortunate enough to brush against them, plants with milky sap that causes blindness, plants with poison bark that produces wounds similar to thermal burns, and even a plant said to be so toxic that raindrops falling off it causes skin irritation. Walking through the jungle is not a walk in the park.

As difficult as it would be to avoid contact with harmful plants, you will not avoid encounters with insects. We're talking about hornets as big as your thumb (Exodus 23:28), two-inch long stinging ants that travel by the millions, and caterpillars with venom poisonous enough to kill a grown man. This, in addition to the swarms that would love to lay eggs inside your skin, inject disease into your bloodstream, or just swarm about and bite your face, swelling your eyes to the point that you can no longer see. Snakes, poison frogs, spiders, centipedes, and scorpions require no further elaboration. You better know where to sit, sleep, step and pee if you wind up in the jungle.

No problem, you think, just download some info from your smart phone to build a raft and float to safety down the slow-flowing tropical stream. Maybe, but while you're at it, go ahead and download some info on crocodiles, anacondas, piranhas and, oh, what's the name of that one fish? The one that will swim up your stream of urine and lodge itself in your urethra? Better Google that.

We don't have space to talk about quicksand, drug smugglers, hostile tribes and the ever present *tunga*, but you get the idea. My point is this: would you rather have a well-written survival guide or a local trusted guide? Someone who not only grew up in the area, but whose family has resided there going back well before written history? The choice is obvious, whether we are talking about the Amazon Basin or downtown Manhattan, there is no substitute for a trusted guide.

Don't get me wrong, reading up on something is great. This is a powerful first step, not only for traveling in exotic locales, but for becoming a professional rescuer as well. But it is only one step in the maturation process. Yes, you must begin with research. But this must be followed by training, practice, and experience. This will lead you to the final requirement: judgment. And ultimately, it is judgment that will be the deciding factor for whether you survive or perish.

How do you survive long enough to obtain judgment? Relationship. Find someone who already has it and sit at their feet. Listen. Ask questions. Follow the leader. Wisdom comes not from obtaining knowledge, but rather from adapting knowledge to your situation. It's a jungle out there, and if you want to survive, listen to the natives.

Discussion:

1. Like the rappelling example illustrated, trying to perform a critical task with book knowledge alone is foolhardy. What about Bible knowledge alone? Can you think of an example of how "book knowledge" of Scripture lead to a nasty fall?

2. One thing that makes a jungle so dangerous is sensory overload: there is so much to be aware of, so many choices to make. Relate this problem to urban living.

3. Some plants can prove dangerous just by being in their vicinity; so too with people. How do we avoid the dangers of "contact poison" while still following Jesus' example of interacting with sinners?

4. While it is true that competition is fierce in the jungle, so too is cooperation, or as biologists say,

symbiosis. The classic example is the ant colony that feeds on the sap of a tree while at the same time protecting the tree from predators. How do you interact with other "species," with people of other faiths in a symbiotic manner? Is it possible to do so without compromising your beliefs?

5. There are some of God's creatures whose sole purpose seems to be to annoy, mosquitoes being somewhere near the top of the list. For what reason might God have put incredibly annoying people into your life? If you answered, "to teach patience," give a practical step you can take to have a Godly relationship with someone whom you would just as soon direct a can of bug spray at.

6. Choosing a different route of travel, the river as opposed to the forest, may seem like an easier way to travel, but often you are simply exchanging one set of problems for another. Avoiding one path to sin sometimes puts us onto another. For example, distancing yourself from a spouse in order to avoid constant bickering, or spending money you don't have to make a loved one happy. Think of an example from your life and reflect on how best to decide between two paths of hardship.

7. Do you have a spiritual guide in your life? What are the key attributes you look for in a mentor? How does one go about finding a mentor?

8. How do you know if you are ready to become someone's mentor? Is everyone called to men-

tor? If called to be a spiritual mentor, is this something you can consciously prepare for?

9. "Going native" is usually sound advice from a secular survival perspective, but it can get you in trouble from a spiritual perspective. As Christians, we are often called to go against the native way of thinking and acting. It may be a workplace where God's name is thrown about in vain or where gossip is the lunch-time norm. What should we do when the cultural norm goes against our beliefs, especially when we are coming onto the scene as a newcomer?

10. Research, Training, Practice, Experience, Judgment. These are great steps to maturity. But how does it equate to your Christian walk? How can you take a step down this jungle trail?

XVII

ANALOGY OF THE CITY: LIFE IN THE HERD

> I will surely gather all of you, O Jacob; I will surely bring together the remnant of Israel. I will bring them together like sheep in a pen, like a flock in its pasture; the place will throng with people.
>
> Micah 2:12

One of the first things you learn about in 9th grade social studies class is something called the Neolithic Revolution. Turns out that some thousands of years ago people decided to stop roaming around hunting mammoths and gathering nuts and roots, and take up residence in some comfortable-looking river valley, like the Nile or the Tigris-Euphrates. Staying in one spot was a big deal, because now it made sense to grow crops and herd livestock rather than hunt and gather. Permanent residences allowed people to accumulate wealth and specialize in one particular occupation or craft. And the accumulation of wealth and the concentration of craftsmen meant an increase in trade, which of course required a transportation network, a protecting army and a monetary system, all of which required a written language, government and, you guessed it, taxes. Thus began the rise of cities.

There are a lot of advantages to city-life. Having grown up in a mid-size city, I had access to a wide array of sporting events, museums, parks, music venues, learning institutions, and cultural opportunities. If I wanted to, I could have partaken in a different activity every weekend of the year. But the vast majority of people who move to cities don't do so to watch baseball games and stroll through art galleries, they do so to escape poverty.

Rural poverty is not a pretty sight. America has its fair share of run-down trailer parks, failed farms, half-abandoned coal mining communities and struggling Indian reservations. It is heartbreaking to witness the results of third and fourth generation poverty tucked away in the hills of Appalachia or the backwaters of Mississippi, but it is even more sobering to realize that America is the richest country on the planet, and one only need to cross a political border or take a hop across a body of water to see rural poverty in its true fury.

Country folk starve to death. They walk behind water buffalo hoping to pick a few grains of half-digested seeds from the dung which drops on dirt trails. They lack sanitation, drinking from visibly dirty rivers which do double-duty as drinking fountains and open latrines. Rural peasants labor all day in the life-sapping heat, as opportunistic parasites bore eagerly through their bare feet in order to lay thousands of eggs that will hatch into life-sapping intestinal worms. They die from childbirth, malaria, tuberculosis, typhoid, tetanus, measles, dehydration and malnutrition. Given such prospects, is it any wonder that many look to the shining lights of the big city as a panacea for the problems they face? Move to the city, find a job, save your money, send for your family, create a brighter future. It is a dream as old as the Neolithic Revolution.

Man is a social creature. If you doubt this, drive down any stretch of highway that you choose and watch the traffic flow. Regardless of speed limit or traffic conditions, there will always be an intense effort to stay as closely as possible to the person in front. It's as true for zebras as it is for urbanites: don't get separated from the herd. In a city the opportunities for social connection abound. Instead of being betrothed to your second cousin at the age of seven, you now have the opportunity to interact with hundreds, or even thousands of potential mates. Instead of the limitations of tribal affiliation, you can now freely intermingle with a plethora of cultures, races, religions, and nationalities. And although the Internet has eroded this truth to a large degree, it is still true to say that nowhere is social interaction greater than in the city.

With so many people in one place, problems are likely to arise (Genesis 3:5-7). City managers have known this for millennia and have planned accordingly. There are professionally trained people to handle every hazard that might arise in urban living: firefighters stand ready, police patrol regularly and ambulances respond 24/7. Every large city has a small army of social workers, rehab centers, civic organizations, sanitation workers, sewer and water authority staff, power and gas personnel to handle the needs of city dwellers. With jobs, entertainment, social opportunity and an army of professional caretakers, there are indeed wonderful benefits to city life. That being said, there is no more dangerous place on earth to live than the city.

It is true that you are far less likely to starve to death in a city or die from lack of prompt medical care. It is equally true that you are far more likely to be shot. Or stabbed, or mugged, or raped, or robbed, or extorted. The very sociability factor that attracts people to cities can quickly take a negative turn. "Herd mentality" too easily degenerates into "Mob mentality" (Matthew 27:15-26). After thousands of years of city dwelling, we are still exploring the ramifications of living in close proximity to so many, of being exposed to constant noise, light and interaction, never being able to retreat to a "quiet place."

It's great that cities have infrastructure in place to deal with urban problems, but the flip-side of the coin is that this infrastructure is a *necessity* to survival itself, and when it breaks down, the very lives of urban dwellers are at risk. All it takes is one blizzard, flood, tornado, hurricane, riot, strike, gas leak, train wreck, power outage, terrorist strike or pandemic to turn a blossoming city into a killing field. I will not even delve into the fact that most American cities of any substantial size are listed as a target site for thermonuclear bombs, at which point infrastructure becomes a chillingly moot point...

Jobs? Yes, cities provide millions of employment opportunities for hard-working occupants. They also offer a marketplace for prostitutes, drug dealers, extortionists, organized crime, child laborers and human trafficking. These professions in turn, create unlimited job opportunities for emergency rooms, rehabilitation centers, welfare offices, detention facilities, law enforcement, child protective services, and mortuaries. The lights of a city are evocative and entrancing from afar. Drive through the inner parts of a city at night and the glow of neon might prove far less attractive (c.f. Proverbs 7:6-23).

This social filth is not the only pollution present in the city. There is also the very real health hazard of environmental pollution. Smog is part of everyday life for more and more urbanites, contributing to unprecedented levels of asthma, lung cancer and respiratory complications. Paving the planet may have reduced malaria-infested swamps and trichinosis worms, but living in close proximity with millions of others, residing in energy efficient homes that are becoming more and more "airtight," and being exposed to an incredible array of chemicals, energies, and particulates on a daily basis isn't much better. Every time we try to combat one problem-asbestos, lead paint, open sewers, another pops up in its place- radon, sink holes, acid rain. In nature, when a group of communal animals consume all the resources in an area or contaminate the surroundings with waste, they move on. What option for the city dweller?

It would be easy to declare the urban life a stronghold of sin and despair. It would also be easy to argue that cities are filled with wonderful opportunities and services and have become a necessity on a planet of 7 billion humans, each with very real physical and social needs. Such a debate is not the goal or within the scope of this text. Our concern is survival, and as such, we must ponder on how the principles of survival apply to any realm we find ourselves in and what skills will be required to survive. Every place we reside in, be it desert or mountain, open waters or city streets, requires a set of general and specific survival skills. But here is what makes city survival unique and here is what will drive many of our survival decisions: nowhere else are we more likely to encounter others in dire need of rescue than on the streets of a city (Matthew 23:37).

Discussion:

1. What skills are crucial for an urban survivor that might not be as necessary for the wilderness survivor?

2. The Bible portrays cities as places of great evil, as in Sodom, Gomorrah and Ninevah. But it also speaks of the Holy City, a New Jerusalem, and a City on the Hill. Taken as a whole, do you see cities as a blessing or a curse in today's world?

3. The same crowd that cried, Hosannah! and waved palm branches in homage to Jesus

became the crowd that cried, Crucify Him! How could this happen over the space of a few days? What does this say about human nature? How can we protect ourselves from being part of a mob mentality?

4. Cities have allowed people to specialize in a specific trade or skill. What specific skills do you have that you can bring to the Christian community?

5. Pollution is any substance that is concentrated to the point of being harmful. What spiritual pollutants are in your life? What does it mean to spiritually clean up? What does it mean to move on to a cleaner environment?

6. What does it mean when Jesus speaks of Himself as having no permanent dwelling (Luke 9:58)? Are you called to this?

7. What are the advantages of living in a community of believers? Disadvantages?

8. Disaster results in the breakdown of services. As Christians, how do we prepare our families for this possibility?

9. If Jesus often retreated to a quiet place, why don't more people go on retreats? How do you go on a retreat in the midst of a noisy, sinful situation?

PART IV:

FROM SURVIVOR TO RESCUER

> My prayer is not that you take them out of the world but that you protect them from the evil one.
>
> John 17:15

What images come to mind when you picture a rescue squad? Do you picture a firefighter rushing out of an inferno with a child cradled in arm? A National Guardsmen rappelling from a helicopter toward a raging river? Or maybe a nurse bringing an aura of calm to a scene of utter chaos. Whatever the case, we recognize these occupations as being noble and selfless. These are individuals who have dedicated themselves to the safety of others, even if it means going in harm's way.

In my youth I often dreamed of being a rescuer. What is more appealing than overcoming some horrendous danger in a courageous manner, of hearing the cheers of a grateful public, and receiving the kisses and embraces of the rescued (funny how in my daydreams the only people requiring rescue were beautiful young women). As wonderful as such scenarios appeared in my youth, the truth of the matter is far more fantastic and far less egocentric: we *are* called to be part of a rescue squad. Each of us plays an important role in an elite organization of highly dedicated truly motivated rescue workers. Our mission is paramount, our equipment cutting-edge. The training is as rigorous and realistic as you want to make it, and the call alert rings on a daily basis. Every survivor has the chance to become a rescuer.

XVIII

THE RESCUE STATION

Be my rock of refuge, to which I can always go;
give the command to save me, for you are my
rock and my fortress.

Psalm 71:3

Every rescue organization has a base from which to
operate out of. These can be well-established structures like hospitals or fire stations, replete with top notch equipment, communication consoles, modern living quarters and dining facilities. A base can also be mobile and temporary, like a MASH unit or military Forward Operating Base, difficult to distinguish from the chaos and danger just outside the base perimeter. But despite the degree of complexity and permanence, every base has this in common: it provides rescuers with an increased sense of stability and control, and even more important, a heightened sense of family. To witness an example of this you need go no farther than your neighborhood fire station...

The fire station I visited was in a local suburb of Rochester, NY, but it could have been any town in America. Across the street from the local school, nestled among small businesses, and prominently flying the national and state flag in front, the station is consciously designed to be an integral part of the community: rescuers live amongst us.

We are welcomed by a smiling member of the department, whose sharply creased pants and well-polished shoes are telling examples of the pride she takes in her organization. The plaques on the wall of the front hall echo this sentiment: they are reminders that this department has done great things in the past and the expectation is of great things to come.

Everywhere there is the sense of mission, most evident by a prominent motto emblazed upon the wall. Elite units often try to summarize their beliefs in a single, poignant statement:

> To Free the Oppressed.
> Army Special Forces
> You have to go out, but you do not have to come back.
> Coast Guard rescue swimmers
> That Others May Live.
> Air Force Pararescue.

It is far more than a catch phrase or Latin sound bite. To those who wear the shirt or sport the ball cap with this motto, it truly is a mission statement and way of life.

How dedicated these folks are is most deeply expressed by the framed portraits below the motto. It is in remembrance of comrades who have fallen in the course of duty. The faces are all smiling, bright and eager. The eyes say it all: we are here to serve. We understand the risk. Here I am. Below each portrait is a name and dates of service. There is no speaking of agonizing burns, no listing of crushing blows, dizzying falls, or heartless torrents of water. That would be paying lip service to what is not important. I understand the risk. Here I am.

The equipment room proves to be the most popular part of the tour. I am touring with a group of teenaged students, who laugh as they try to move about with heavy turnout coats and oxygen bottles placed upon their backs. We all smile and plug our ears at the sound of the helmet distress siren; it automatically activates when a firefighter has stopped moving for sixty seconds. Locator beacons, Kevlar, Nomex, AEDs…there is a sense of power and control. We have already forgotten the lesson in sacrifice from the front hall (John 15:13).

A quick walk upstairs changes our perspective yet again. Here are the living quarters. Roughly sectioned off are areas for rest, exercise and recreation. Rescue workers are not merely knights in Nomex armor; they are our flesh and blood neighbors. Heroes must sleep. Heroes watch goofy television shows and play foosball. Heroes must eat, and when given a choice, firefighters will always gather about in a family atmosphere to eat. There is no hired hand, everyone takes their turn at preparing meals (and critiquing those who do). And it is in this breaking of bread that bonds of brotherhood are formed, bonds that may quite literally be tested in fire (Luke 24:30).

Yes, there is a fire pole, and yes, there is a child-like rush in sliding down it. The captain and his lieutenant greet us below, perhaps smiling in welcome, or perhaps chuckling at how awkwardly we make our descent. He explains how every member of the force is part of a team. Everyone has a job to do, be it operating a hose or pump, entering structures, administering first aid or coordinating with other departments (1Corinthians 12:14). Everyone knows the chain of command, so there is a sense of order from the white-helmeted captain all the way down to the orange-helmeted rookie. If one falls, another will step in to take their place. And when the captain tells us that each member of the department places their very lives in the hands of one another, each and every member of the department spontaneously and gravely nods their head in agreement. I am left with a lump in my throat. You have to go out, but you do not have to come back.

We exited the station through the large bay doors. Immaculate red and silver trucks stand at the ready. The drive in front is marked and cleared like the deck of an aircraft carrier. Turnout clothes hang at the ready. When I stood at the end of the drive, staring at the massive silver frame of a pumper truck, watching the relaxed-yet-alert manner of the on-duty crew, I was struck with insight behind the meaning of a rescue base. Everything we had witnessed-from the high-tech equipment room, to the shiny brass pole, to the pot of boiling spaghetti in the common kitchen, to the young recruit scrubbing hubcaps even now- everything was purposely designed for one thing and one thing only:

when that bell rings, when our neighbors cry for help, we will go. We will drop every comfort and convenience of daily living, we will leave every normalcy of this house, and we will go. Not after hours of reflection, not after minutes of debate. In the space of mere seconds, we will depart the safety of this base and rush into whatever hazards may be. And God-willing, when the crisis is over and the flames are quenched, the bandages applied, we will return to the safety of this house (Ephesians 6:13). We will service our gear, rest, laugh and share bread with our companions. We will mourn the fallen, rejoice in the company of the living, and always stand ready for the next rescue. Here I am.

Discussion:

1. What does it mean to have a spiritual base of operations?
2. Most rescue organizations are organized into tiers (international, national, state, county, etc.). From a spiritual perspective, what are the advantages to this approach? disadvantages?
3. Churches often have community outreaches that in our analogy can be thought of as Forward Operations Bases (FOB): usually mobile and temporary. What are the advantages to this approach? disadvantages?
4. Do you feel called to participate in an FOB? Have you considered starting a new one?
5. How a church ornaments itself is a visual expression of its approach to ministry. Cross or cru-

cifix? Changes with liturgical seasons? Paying reverence through artwork and precious materials? Declaring union with the poor through lack of comfort items? What message does your building send to visitors?

6. Uniforms are meant to encourage a sense of identity and mission. What message do you want your spiritual team to express through clothing?

7. What is the mission statement of your church/ team? Is it important to have one? Is it important that members can verbalize this to others?

8. The Church has always had heroes: saints, leaders, and perhaps most powerful, martyrs. How should your team honor and remember such heroes? When does honoring a hero of the faith cross the line and become a form of idolatry?

9. Does your church have a chain of command? Is this a source of tension or of comfort? What happens when you are in disagreement with leadership?

10. Is your team ready to respond to spiritual emergencies in a timely manner? Are there immediate action drills in place, well communicated and regularly rehearsed? Debriefings?

XIX

RECRUITMENT

"MEN WANTED: FOR HAZARDOUS JOURNEY. SMALL WAGES, BITTER COLD, LONG MONTHS OF COMPLETE DARKNESS, CONSTANT DANGER, SAFE RETURN DOUBTFUL. HONOUR AND RECOGNITION IN CASE OF SUCCESS. SIR ERNEST SHACKLETON"

London Times

It is difficult to determine how a man will react under duress, and survival tales abound with surprises. Why is it that experienced soldiers, well trained and equipped, cracked under pressure and rushed blindly into a jungle where they turned on each other and perished? How did a teen-aged girl, wearing little more than high heels and a mini-skirt survive a plane crash in the Amazon and ten days later walks out alive, the sole survivor? Determining who is a good candidate for survival is difficult enough, but we are taking the question to the next level: who will make a good candidate for a rescuer?

Suppose you were in charge of putting together an elite team with the purpose of accomplishing a dangerous assignment. Each member will be subjected to incredible trials in the course of which physical, mental and spiritual weaknesses will likely result in the collapse of the entire mission. Success will result in eternal glory; failure will equate to a cold and agonizing death. Now, how do you put together your crew? This was the task that faced famed explorer Sir Ernest Shackleton in 1914. At a time when Europe was preparing for a war of unthinkable proportions, he was preparing to execute his own unthinkable task: the first crossing of the Antarctic continent.

The immensity of this expedition is mindboggling. Even to get to Antarctica required the precision, resources and daring of a military expedition, at a time when the British military was more concerned about German invasion than traipsing across the most barren spot on the planet. Any flaw in navigation, resupply, communication, meteorology, or leadership would surely result in failure and likely result in death; and death in the polar regions could manifest itself in a myriad of frozen hells, none of which are pretty. Previous attempts at polar expedition had resulted in deaths by drowning, starvation, carbon monoxide poisoning, attack by polar bear, killer whale and leopard seal, hypothermia, frostbite, and falling into bottomless crevasses. Other causes of death remain unknown because the bodies have never been found, although some speculate that this was partially due to cannibalism.

None of this was news to Shackleton. He had led numerous expeditions before, and he knew what was required of a man, and a team, to return successfully

(Micah 6:8). He would only have the resources to support a small group, perhaps twenty five, so it would be critical that each man exhibit competence in a critical skill, and preferably be proficient in multiple areas. Dog handlers, sailors, medics, hunters, navigators, photographers, meteorologists, engineers, physicists, geologists, artists-all would have to perform their duties to near-perfection.

Of course, competence is only one part of the equation. It is all well and good for a man to declare himself to be a highly competent mechanic, but how will he react if a whale rams the ship and icy water begins swirling about his thighs? What will he do if he has lost half his fingers to frostbite and his bunkmate is so hungry that he begs to bite off the blackened flesh for a meal? What will be his mental state when he is told that the ship has been crushed by ice floes and they will be forced to winter in temperatures in excess of 80 degrees below zero? Such things happen on polar expeditions, and the mettle of a man is all that stands between survival and death.

Shackleton knew that he needed more than brave men, he needed bold men. The difference? A survivor needs bravery; a rescuer needs boldness. A survivor is thrust into dire circumstances without consent. Fear is present and cannot be ignored, but a survivor must see fear for what it is, and then be able to master it. Psychologists tell us that 80-90 percent of people are unable to think clearly in a crisis and the tendency is to freeze when action is required the most. Bravery is the ability to override this tendency, or even better, to channel fear in a positive manner, to use the flood of hormones as an asset.

Boldness ups the ante. It is a conscious decision to place yourself in a situation where bravery is required; it is a choice. A professional rescuer must not only be bold, but must be habitually so, must make boldness a habit. Think of the rescue workers who rushed into the World Trade Center while others rushed out and you will have a bittersweet example of what it means to be bold. Bravery is a response; boldness is a decision.

With boldness comes confidence, but the confidence of a rescuer must not be limited to self- confidence. Belief in self alone devolves into arrogance and an inflation of self-importance and ability, and this becomes an illusion of reality. People who see only what they want to see, what they expect to see, place themselves squarely in the danger zone. Make no mistake: the surest way to become a victim of crisis is to fail to see the reality of what is before you. So when we speak of confidence necessary for a rescuer, we are speaking of confidence in self, yes, but also a confidence in teammates, leaders, mission and God.

A rescuer must be sacrificial (Romans 12:1). As soon as self supersedes service, a rescuer slips back into the role of survivor, and if not careful, may even descend into the undesirable position of victim. Sacrifice means giving up personal gain and comfort for the sake of another, and here is what makes sacrifice so difficult for people to swallow: real sacrifice leads to suffering. There is no way around this, which is why a truly sacrificial person is at once both rare and admirable. A sacrificial nature might be rare, but it is mandatory for those who bear the mantle of leadership. Shackleton exemplified this time and again in his role of expedition leader, but perhaps it is most poignantly expressed when he offered his mittens to a suffering shipmate, resulting in eternal gratitude from the shipmate and permanent frostbite for Shackleton. Encapsulated in this miniscule moment is a message of sacrifice that every adventurer who wishes to become rescuer must embrace: service over self.

Finally, a virtue that embraces all others for the rescuer: self-control (1Peter 1:13). Without self-control at the scene of a crisis, rescuer number one becomes victim number two. For it is self-control that provides a person with the discipline necessary to master a skill when distractions abound; self-control that allows a rescuer to channel fear into productive energy; self-control that restrains a bold spirit from becoming a reckless liability; and self-control that allows one to forego immediate gratification and comfort in order to sacrificially provide for the needs of others. Each and every member of Shackleton's team mastered self-control. This is how they survived 497 days adrift on an ice floe without the loss of a single man.

If you are looking for candidates for a rescue squad, the example of Shackleton's leadership and the crew he forged is worthy of considerable study, but if you are unable to study the exploits of this man, remember this: competence, courage, boldness, sacrifice, self-control.

Discussion:

1. How did Christ recruit members of His rescue squad?

2. It has been said that God is not so much interested in our ability as our availability. When putting together a ministry team how important is a person's competence as compared to a person's willingness to serve?

3. What are some of the challenges and dangers that a modern missionary team might face?

4. Think of a church outreach that is important to you. What are some of the desirable practical skills necessary for this outreach team to have? Spiritual skills?

5. What are the top 3-5 traits you would look for when recruiting a team for ministry?

6. How well did Christ's disciples exhibit the character traits above?

7. Can a man be taught to be courageous? How do you teach someone to overcome fear?

8. How do we "advertise" for bold men of action to service the Church?

9. What prevents a man from having self-control?

10. Jesus serves as our example of character and leaves us with the Holy Spirit to strengthen our resolve. He also sends men and women into our lives as fleshly examples of how to live. Next to each character trait below write down the name of someone in your life who exemplifies this trait.

Competence:
Courage:
Boldness:
Sacrifice:
Self-Control:

11. In a moment of prayer, ask that you might be strengthened in one of the areas. Pray that you might eagerly answer the advertisement Christ has put out for the recruitment of adventurous souls. Then hang on for what very well might be the ride of your life.

XX

TRAINING

We do not rise to the level of our expectations,
we rise to the level of our training.

—Archilochuse

There is not an organization, team or unit in the world
that could not be improved through quality training,
that is to say training with a clear purpose, conducted
with realism, progressive in nature, with honest feedback throughout. Unfortunately, anybody who has been
around the corporate, military, educational or missionary world will tell you the same thing: too often we
receive the training but forego the quality. A poorly
conceived and executed training program leads to a
decrease in morale, a stagnation in competence and a
resentment toward leadership. A well-planned and executed training program creates esprit de corps, practical
skills improvement, and a hunger to excel. Such was the
training I received at Ranger School.

US Army Ranger School has seen several modifi-
cations over the decades, but its goal has always been
the same: train leaders to be proficient in small-unit
tactics under combat conditions anywhere in the world.

For me this journey began in 1988 when I and my fellow wet-behind-the-ears infantry lieutenants marched under a large "Ranger" sign at Fort Benning, Georgia. A Ranger Instructor (RI) politely strode up to us and began in a low voice, "You are now in Ranger country, and in Ranger country YOU RUN!" The last bellow jolted us into a double-time pattern that would last for the next eight weeks.

The first item we were issued was the Ranger Handbook. This pocket-sized manual became our sacred scripture for all things Ranger: demolitions, raids, ambushes, recons, helicopter operations, rappelling and parachuting…all the details that we were likely to forget under moments of extreme duress could be found in the handbook. And the first item listed was the Ranger Creed. Committed to memory, it reminded us who we were, where we came from, and what our mission was. It begins with, "Recognizing that I volunteered as a Ranger, fully knowing the hazards of my chosen profession," and ends with, I will "fight on to the Ranger objective and complete the mission, though I be the lone survivor." (Ranger Handbook). Everything that followed in the manual, everything we learned for the next two months were mere details of this purpose.

If you want to train for the rigors of combat, you have to be prepared to be uncomfortable (or as my commander in Alaska put it, You can't teach Arctic concepts to a warm man). And so our instructors did their best to simulate combat conditions: night rappels down two- hundred- foot cliffs, sometimes with casualties strapped to our backs; parachuting from helicopters with full combat loads into deserts and mountains; swamp patrols culminating in live-fire ambushes; low crawling in what can best be described as sewer waste with barbed wire, affectionately known as "the worm pit." Interlaced with an endless array of road marches, obstacle courses, land navigation and physical miseries, sometimes planned, sometimes provided courtesy of an unpredictable Mother Nature. Realistic training, conducted with intensity, saves lives ("The more we sweat in peace, the less we bleed in war." –Sun Tzu.).

Despite the chaotic maelstrom it felt like at the time, our training was carefully planned to be progressive in nature (1 Corinthians 3:2) We crawled before we ran (although I seem to remember doing a lot of crawling *and* a lot of running!). Hours were spent learning knots and rope work before we flung ourselves off of cliff faces; ambush operations were practiced for days before we locked and loaded thirty- round magazines of 5.56 ball and tracer ammo and fired into the night; even the proper method of slaughtering a chicken was rehearsed before we tried it on our own, as the RI's "pet" alligators watched on in anticipation. If you were able to overcome the effects of sleep deprivation and acute hunger long enough to actually focus on what was being taught, every skill was broken down into a learnable, progressive format.

The key phrase here is "overcome the effects of sleep deprivation and acute hunger." Funny things happen when you average three hours of sleep on two "meals" a day for extended periods of time. I remember a ranger buddy trying to put a quarter into a tree, thinking it was a soda machine; people seeing beautiful girls in white dresses carrying baskets of cookies, grown men ready to engage in a fist fight over the ownership of a portion of saltine cracker; planning a reconnaissance raid on an air force dumpster, hoping to find some scraps from their mess hall without being caught by the RIs. I remember spending an entire twelve mile march through the Georgia mountains thinking of nothing but how fine it would be to eat a double Whopper and fries. I lost so much weight that it hurt to sit (no padding). I lost so much sleep that I slept through a full-scale live-fire ambush. The more we sweat in peace...

Communication is critical between a trainer and trainee, and in Ranger School here's how it worked: Throughout the course we were under constant evaluation. RIs would frequently and spontaneously reassign leadership positions, meaning everybody had to know the plan, know where we were, know the state of the unit...in short, be ready to live up to the Ranger motto: Rangers lead the way. There was no room for gray areas; every task, every patrol was either a GO or a NO GO. After every rotation, the RIs would sit down with student leaders and debrief. Details were given, advice was offered, and usually second chances were available.

In addition, peer evaluations were also made, and this could be extremely nerve wracking. Ranger candidates came from all units of the armed forces and included troops from US allies around the world. National and unit loyalties and prejudices could mean a bad peer review for inconsequential reasons: "We don't want to lose anyone from our home unit, so we will give negative reviews to those in rival units." It was yet another stressor in a stress-filled environment, as a series of poor reviews could mean being recycled back to the beginning of the course (referred to as going to the Gulag) or even being dropped from training. This fear of failure, lack of sleep, and the disparity of power between RIs and Ranger candidates could all serve as obstacles to open dialogue; perhaps realistic in a combat environment, but not ideal for quality training.

Half of those we started with were not standing with us on graduation day (Matthew 25:32). On this day a group of bald-headed, emaciated young men slept on their feet as they waited to receive the visual symbol of their completion. And as we were called to attention, the RIs came forward with our "diploma," a pinky-sized black and yellow patch with the word, "Ranger" scrolled across it. Our training was complete, but now the real task would begin. As Ranger graduates we were expected to return to our parent units and supervise the training of others- training with a clear purpose, conducted with realism, progressive in nature, with honest feedback throughout. We were expected to continue our skills development and remain on the cutting edge of small unit tactics. And when the call came, we were to "fight on to the Ranger objective and complete the mission, though I be the lone survivor." Rangers Lead the Way.

Discussion:

1. Like the Ranger Handbook, people refer to the Holy Bible as a life manual. This is a great sound bite, but how do you apply it? What is a practical suggestion you can give someone for using the Bible as a life manual?

2. The early Church formulated several creeds as a way of summarizing the beliefs of the Church (the Nicene Creed and the Apostles Creed most notably). Some denominations recite these regularly and encourage memorization, others ignore them entirely. Is there value in studying and memorizing church creeds?

3. "You can't teach Arctic concepts to a warm man." Do you agree with this statement? How does it apply to training for ministry?

4. "You must learn to crawl before you learn to run" is a basic tenet of human development. Can you think of a biblical example that confirms or contradicts this?

5. No Christian would dispute the importance of regular prayer, it is sanctioned again and again in the Bible. Yet, so is fasting, a practice all but extinct in many church communities. Why is there almost a taboo against fasting in today's culture? What are the spiritual benefits of depriving your body of food and/or sleep?

6. Saint Paul never held back in his letters to church communities. He praised with gusto and he condemned with gusto. In a world where

most ministries are staffed by volunteers, it can prove difficult for church leaders to have honest communication with their staff because of the fear of hurting feelings or driving away well-meaning individuals. What advice would you give a pastor who wishes to improve honest communication?

7. The first lesson of Ranger School was this: never leave your buddy. Those who couldn't immediately point out the location of their buddy were made to gallop around the training area screaming, "Lone Ranger! Lone Ranger!" Who is your Ranger buddy? What is their spiritual location? If you hesitate in answering these questions, something is amiss…

8. Half of Ranger candidates don't graduate. Sad, perhaps, but here is the true tragedy: Half of all marriages fail. Half of young Christians leave the Church. What can *you* do about this?

9. Graduating Ranger School is kind of like being baptized/confirmed: Yes, it is a fantastic event, but now the expectation is that you will continue your personal training and you will bring what you learn into the lives of others. What steps are you taking to continue your spiritual growth? How are you bringing what you learn into the lives of others?

10. When a ranger salutes an officer, he says, "Rangers lead the way," to which the officer replies, "All the way." It is a statement that goes back to D-Day in World War II, and it affirms

the belief that a Ranger doesn't wait to be told what needs to be done. He is expected to lead without hesitation. Play with this phrase for a bit: "Christians lead the way." Is it true? Should it be? Is it true for you?

XXI

EQUIPMENT

The mettle of a man is reflected in the metal of
his sword.

—Blomgren

A half-dozen survival instructors gathered around a
campfire to shoot the breeze, and as they did so the
topic of conversation turned thus: if you could carry
one piece of survival gear into the wild, what would it
be and why? The first instructor said a knife, because he
wanted protection. The next said a fire-maker, because
he wanted comfort. The third said a signal mirror,
because he wanted to be saved. The fourth said a compass, because he wanted a sense of direction. And the
fifth said a survival manual, because he wanted to have
a plan. When it came time for the final instructor to
respond, he paused for a moment and said, "The Bible."
Silence. Asked why, his response: "Because I want to
have everything mentioned by the others."

If you want to see a lively debate, get onto these
websites that declare: Ten essential items for your survival kit. A lot of good advice interspersed with a lot of
comments from bored, deranged amateurs. But we're

beyond survival kits at this point; we want to know about putting together a rescue kit. This means not only protecting ourselves but being prepared to come to the aid of others. It means considering mission, encumbrance, maintenance, and quality.

As always, consider mission first. What are you trying to do, with whom, for whom, under what conditions? The gear required by a horse-mounted search-and-rescue deputy will differ from a swift-water rescue technician will differ from a member of the ski patrol. Mission parameters to consider include: weather and terrain elements, friendly and enemy forces, time frames, available resources, extraction plans, etc. It is not foolish to have a "go-bag" ready for any situation, but knowing mission parameters will greatly facilitate what gets packed and what stays home.

Encumbrance refers to how difficult something is to carry. How heavy is it? How much weight? How much space? Encumbrance is directly related to the means of carrying an object. In your pocket? A vehicle or pack animal? A backpack? The question of encumbrance limits what and how something will be available.

In considering how to carry your gear, think in terms of concentric circles. The inner circle includes those items that will be physically on your body at all times. When you are drowning in a river or being swept away by an avalanche, most of your gear will quickly be discarded. Stripping down at a base camp will also see items set aside. But there are certain things that should be carried on your body at all times during a rescue operation. These inner circle items might include a neck knife, a wrist compass, first-aid compress, para-cord bracelet…items that are more survival-oriented than rescue-oriented. Choosing not to carry these items will put your life unnecessarily at risk, rendering you useless in helping others.

Next to consider are those items that will be carried in packs. Extensive first-aid supplies, extraction devices, alpine gear and camp gear might fall into this category. As much as possible, try to disperse mission-critical equipment between multiple team members and packs. This lowers the chances that the mission will fail on account of the loss of one bag.

The outer circle of gear is what is brought but not physically carried by you. It might be towed in a trailer, kept on a boat, towed on an ahkio sled or strapped to your horse. These are items too bulky, delicate or com-munal in nature to hand carry, and might include items like cookware, a triage tent, jaws of life, or oxygen tanks. Because of this, your means of transportation will dra-matically determine rescuer comfort and rescue options.

How much can be carried is directly related to user preference and physical conditioning (1Samuel 17:38). My rule for family backpacking is simple: you can bring whatever you want so long as you are willing to carry it. Many others follow this same philosophy, as I have seen mountaineers break out champagne glasses and cham-pagne at the 14,410 summit of Mount Rainier and had a First Sergeant who, three days into a desert patrol pulled a twelve- pound watermelon out of his rucksack.

That's cool, but as a member of a rescue squad things are a little different. For the sake of mission performance, the team must collaborate on who carries what. Repetition of items can result in unnecessary weight, slowing down the entire rescue. Everybody doesn't need their own sixty- meter mainline rope, camp stoves and individual tooth paste tubes. When seconds and ounces count, every item, be it comfort or mission essential, needs to be coordinated at the team level. This includes ensuring that everyone knows where you carry your personal first aid kit and medications.

Next to consider is maintenance. Poorly maintained equipment promotes questionable performance, something that a rescuer can never afford. While many rescue squads have a maintenance plan in place, the weak link can sometimes lie with personal equipment. Sure, you regularly inspect the team's ropes, but what about your boot laces, saddle cinch and helmet strap? It's funny how we can get so concerned with helping the team that we neglect ourselves and ultimately are a detriment to the team anyway. Two ways to prevent this? An idiot-proof personal equipment checklist and a buddy who's finickier than you are.

Field maintenance is equally important. Items that break, go out of calibration, suck battery power, leak, or shy away from moisture need TLC, and if this can't be provided under field conditions, maybe it's best to replace them or leave them at home. You can always pick out a professional rescuer. He's the guy that looks after his horse/rifle/rope first while all the wannabes are focused on hot chow and cat naps. And post-mission maintenance? If you don't recognize the importance of this, please don't respond to the call.

As a rule of thumb, always buy the best equipment that you can afford. Note: the best equipment doesn't necessarily mean the newest or the most expensive. Ask yourself questions like: will this item withstand the beating I am likely to put it through? Am I willing to carry and maintain this item when everything goes south? Does this serve a team need that is not currently being met? Do I want one tool that does many things in a mediocre fashion or several tools that do one thing well? Would I risk my mother's life on the performance of this item?

When it comes to equipment, there are two extremes that can get you into trouble very quickly:

1) not being familiar enough with your gear and
2) becoming overly-dependent on it (Psalm 20:17).

You must know your gear, inside and out, and a rescue mission is not the time for breaking in unfamiliar gear. Read the manual, practice with it under combat conditions, keep a maintenance journal, so that when the time comes you are intimately familiar with the capabilities of your gear.

And finally, do not become overwhelmed should your gear become lost, malfunction or be sitting in the wrong go-bag. History is filled with people in dire straits just like yours who have done far more with far less. I leave you with one example: An elderly Inuit woman, with nothing but the clothes on her back, was confronted by a hungry polar bear that rushed upon her, jaws gaping and moving in to eat her. She rapidly plunged her hand in and out of the beast's mouth.

The bear was later found dead, suffocated with an arctic mitten shoved deep in its throat.

Discussion:

1. If you were told to be prepared to go on a rescue mission, what one piece of gear would you be sure to pack? Your second choice? Why?
2. What is the most likely rescue scenario you can see yourself engaged in? Given this scenario, what should you have packed and ready to go at all times?
3. Christ instructs His followers to take no gear with them as they go about their mission (Luke 9:3). What is the message for us behind this?
4. Sometimes what we think we are carrying to help us is actually hurting us. For example, a firefighter wearing his boots and coat in a raging river. What is something in your life that is encumbering you? What is preventing you from setting it down?
5. Some things in life are too heavy to carry by yourself, yet are crucial to the mission. Who helps you carry such loads? How are such loads balanced?
6. What kind of spiritual maintenance do you perform under normal conditions, back in "garrison?" Does this get neglected when things get tough in the field? What about after the mission has been completed?

7. What kind of specialized gear or skill do you bring to the team? What would be your dream piece of equipment or skill?

8. In story we often read of a hero being given a special piece of gear by the powers that be. Perseus received his sword and shield, Luke got his first light saber, Jimmy Olson got his Superman signaling watch, etc. In reality, God gives us all a gift to be used for His purposes (1Corinthians 12). Have you made yourself intimately familiar with this piece of equipment? Are you using it as God intends?

9. Is there anything or anyone in your life that you have become overly dependent upon?

10. What has been a time in your life that your gear has failed you? Think literally first (the rope broke, the car died, the alarm didn't go off). What were the results? Now think symbolically (I couldn't patch up a relationship, my talents fell short, I made a bad judgment call). What were the results? Was maintenance an issue in the equipment failure?

XXII

RESCUE REJECTED

But you have now rejected your God, who saves
you out of all your calamities and distresses…

1Samuel 10:19

There is a strange paradox that exists in the lore of wilderness survival: people who are lost, people who are injured, even dying, sometimes reject rescue. Perhaps they choose to hide, other times flee. Professional trackers have seen this when searching for those lost in the wild. Sometimes captives will aggressively resist attempts at extraction or even attack would-be rescuers. Such was the case when Army Rangers tried to free American POWs from a Japanese prison camp during WWII. And sometimes they will look a rescuer in the eye and calmly state: I'm not the one that needs rescue; maybe it's you who needs help. Others refuse to abandon a way of life, refusing to evacuate in the midst of a hurricane or oncoming forest fire. And sometimes a would-be rescuer encounters all of the above. Such was the case for the missionaries whose calling took them to the tribes of French Canada.

The Jesuits of the 1700s were the spiritual "commandos" of the Catholic Church. Their degree of theological training, physical toughness and missionary zeal, beginning with their founder Ignatius Loyola, a Spanish military officer, is the stuff of legend. And nowhere did they find greater challenge than deep in the interior of North America. Seen by much of Europe as the abode of the devil, the forests of New France had never heard the name of Jesus-its people living in the darkness of spiritual ignorance- and there were no more highly qualified teachers to dispel this darkness than the Jesuits.

The Huron Indians seemed ripe for rescue to European eyes. They lived in constant fear of attack by the powerful Iroquois of New York State who, thanks to Dutch traders, held the distinction of being the only native group that possessed firearms. The combination of poor soil and bleak Canadian winters meant starvation was an ever-present possibility. The spiritual life of the Huron seemed limited to animal sacrifice, superstition and appeasement of evil spirits, all encouraged and coordinated by the local shaman, seen as little more than a petty scam artist. The entire continent seemed on the verge of spiritual collapse.

The Jesuits, however, were up to the task. They were easily the most well educated men in Europe, masters of rhetoric, language, philosophy, theology, mathematics, physics and metaphysics. They were teachers extraordinaire, founding and staffing universities of the highest caliber. Their training in asceticism- to be in the world but not of the world- prepared them to endure

immense physical hardships and displays of courage, traits which they knew the Indians held in high
regard. Prolific writers and historians, the Jesuits hun-
grily learned everything they could about tribal culture
from their fore-bearers in the New World. Never had a
group of men been so qualified for the role of rescuer;
never had a group of people been in such need of rescue.
Yet, as the black-robed priests made their way into the
settlements and lives of the Huron it quickly became
apparent that something was awry. These people did
not *want* to be rescued, nor feel a *need* to be rescued.

Picture the reaction of a Huron when encountering a missionary priest and his call for salvation: Here's
a man before me who barely qualifies as a man. He
has *hair* on his *face*, like some sort of beast. He wears
a totally impractical garment of feminine nature. He
can't hunt, fish, or even walk through the woods without getting lost. He has utterly no interest in women.
He's too proud to cover himself in mud to keep away
biting insects, too stupid to know that you don't try to
stand up when peeing out of a canoe. At best he is an
infantile, effeminate half-man, at worst he is a demon
who has brought incurable disease, confusion and death
to our home. And yet he speaks of saving us ("Speaks"
is relative; he has been here for years, and we can barely
understand his attempts at language.)

His ideas of a Jesus are interesting; we like much of
his god-son message. We too, welcome peace, holding
all wealth in common, praising the Great Spirit for the
blessings of Creation, and loving one another. We too,
look forward to paradise after death and greater inti-

macy with the Creator. We are sorry this Jesus chose not to come to us personally; he would certainly have been welcome at our council fire. But these Christians? Their priests speak of living one lifestyle, yet their white converts live entirely different. Their interests are limited to fur and shiny metal and the flower of our women. Liquor now flows endlessly into our lodges. Whenever these people appear, disease, conflict and death follow. They have no concept of charity; while one lives in luxury, another starves. They limit themselves to one wife, hold others in bondage, and beat their own children. Even according to their own teachings, it is they, not us, who are in need of salvation.

It is not that the Indians held no respect for the blackrobes. European technology was certainly marvelous and beneficial (here were men who could predict the very motion of the stars and send messages without speaking). They did not covet women, wealth or land as other whites did. And unlike the Protestant efforts at evangelization, the Catholic approach was less stringent in insisting that Indians abandon every aspect of their culture in order to be counted among the saved. Blackrobes taught that you could reject farming, keep your hair long and remain barefoot, yet still be accepted into Paradise.

But perhaps most poignant was the fact that the Jesuit love for their "flock" went to the point of enduring hardship in every form. Not just to the degree of living in native villages and suffering the trials of 17th century forest life, which would cause today's soldiers and professional athletes to collapse in despair, but rather, staying strong in the faith to the point of martyrdom. History tells us of priests who endured being burnt and boiled alive as a form of "baptism." Others had their fingers, ears and skin bitten off, some being forced to eat their own flesh and drink their own blood in mockery of the communion rite. Still others were made to wear stone necklaces. The stones were heated red-hot before being placed on the priest's neck, a perversion of the Rosary necklace. In a warrior society the ability to endure hardship with indifference means everything, and this character displayed by Jesuits was not lost on the Huron.

And at times this expression of love, so reflective of Christ's sacrificial love for us, would bring even the most hardened warrior into accepting baptism, one Huron declaring that though he did not understand the mysteries of reading and writing, the missing fingers of a priest tortured in the "Hell of Iroquoia" were answer to any doubts he formerly had. Through incredibly intense training, unfathomable devotion and unimaginable suffering, the Jesuits brought many to the knowledge and love of Christ.

But here is the historical fact: most rejected the invitation of rescue. And although few Native Americans accepted the European religion or way of life, not a few Frenchmen adopted the Indian lifestyle, choosing to work, live, worship and marry amongst the tribes. How could this be? How could a missionary, acting in accordance with Christ's command to spread the good news to every people and every land, be turned away? How could anyone say no to the gift of eternal life?

How could someone in danger of dying look at his rescuer, smile sadly and reply, "I'm not the one who needs rescuing"? There is perhaps no greater challenge a rescuer must face than wrestling with this reality: rescue is sometimes rejected.

Discussion:

1. People who are choking in a restaurant have been known to shake off help, go off alone into the bathroom, and die. How can you rationally explain this? Why do people deny rescue?

2. A trained rescuer bursts into the room and declares there is great danger inside, evacuate immediately. At the same time, your best friend declares that there is great danger outside, stay put. Who do you listen to? Who do you trust when it comes to spiritual rescue?

3. How do you respond when a missionary from another faith comes to your door and politely suggests that you are on the wrong path to salvation? What is your expectation when you approach someone from a different faith to share your beliefs?

4. Do you believe it important to work out answers ahead of time before discussing your faith? Should you trust that God will give you the proper words to speak, making preparation unnecessary? Is this what Matthew 10:18-20 is saying?

5. What would cause you to seek out a specific person for spiritual instruction? What are you doing in your life that would cause someone to approach you and ask for spiritual instruction?

6. Respond to this argument: It was once acceptable to have multiple wives, like Abraham, Isaac and Jacob did. This made sense to protect women from great depravity and hardship. Later, as culture changed, it became unacceptable. What is morally unacceptable in some cultures is morally acceptable in others, and this is why the Bible must be interpreted by the local community.

7. Should a Christian spend time studying other faiths in order to better understand his own? Would this make evangelization easier? Are there dangers involved?

8. Why do so few American Christians study the lives of Christian martyrs? Why do so few churches encourage this?

9. French missionaries went out to live among the tribes, English missionaries brought tribal members to live with them. Thoughts on this?

10. Who in your life is in need of spiritual rescue? What role are you playing? Is it harder to rescue someone you know or a total stranger?

XXIII

RETURN TO BASE

The survival experience changes you. This is true whether you are on the surviving side of the house or the rescue side. There are a surprising number of survivors out there. Think of the cancer patient, the combat veteran, the graduate of a drug rehab program, the paroled felon. Think of the kid with the alcoholic dad, the guy who lives in the cardboard shack under the highway bridge, the girl who fell victim to date rape.

Fortunately, there are also a surprisingly vast number of rescuers. Think of the firefighter, the sheriff deputy, the American Red Cross worker, the school teacher, the grandmother, the hospital chaplain, the Big Brother volunteer, and the bone marrow donor.

The circumstances of the crisis are as varied as the individuals themselves. However, one thing that every survivor and rescuer is likely to encounter when the crisis has passed is a sense of culture shock. And the ability to process this form of shock, to reflect upon the lessons learned, to overcome the wave of emotions, to connect and reconnect with others will likely prove pivotal in determining whether you return with the identity of survivor or victim. Fear, despair, guilt and self-righteousness are all potential demons that must be conquered as part of the process.

Fear has a way of magnifying our irrational thoughts, robbing us of peace. For example, having survived a powerful earthquake, my heart would pound uncontrollably for years afterward every time the earth vibrated from a passing truck or train. Few people expect to be thrown into a life-threatening crisis, and when it happens there can be a sense of overwhelming fear. Sometimes surviving a trauma can boost confidence: "If I made it through that, I can make it through anything!" The result can be like a broken bone that, once mended, is now denser and stronger than before the break. But the opposite can also occur: "If it happened once, it could happen again, and I am not strong enough to go through such an ordeal again!" The result is more akin to frostbite: you fall prey once, you are more susceptible to getting it again.

Despair will also try to sink its tendrils into the survivor. By its very nature, crisis deprives us of control. We are tossed about on ocean waves, utterly helpless to resist. We are forced to spend the night in hunger, shivering and alone with no choice but to endure until dawn. There is nothing to do but curl up in a ball and wait for our rescuer…or death, whichever comes first. Instead of focusing on what we can do, we dwell on what is beyond our control. Deprived of food, water and sleep, it often behooves the survivor to rest, to be still, but even though you know this is the right thing to do, it can leave one feeling an even greater sense of helplessness. Even after returning to safety, the agony of despair can continue to haunt: what can I cling fast to?

One of the realities of rescue is that everyone doesn't always make it home (Luke 17:34-35). That being the case, those who do make it will likely find themselves facing the agonizing and confusing demon of guilt. Why did I survive where others perished? Could I have done something different to have saved them? Was it my fault that we got into this mess in the first place? How will others look at me? Guilt stems from the premises, "I should have…" and, "I shouldn't have…" Guilt thrives on the mantra of "If."

Upon return from the wilds you will have been exposed to experiences and growth opportunities that many have never experienced. You will look upon old behaviors and cultural norms with a new mindset. Perhaps the survivor will look with disgust at friends who complain about being poor, hungry, or cold. If only they knew the real meaning of these words as you do! And the rescuer is even more likely to fall prey to self-righteousness. What do these "civilians" know about danger? What do they know about rescue? It is a common conundrum: a rescuer must be bold, yet bold is but a half-wavelength separated from conceit.

Spiritual survival and rescue present the exact same dilemmas as physical survival. Those who have been saved through the grace of God, those who have participated in Christ's rescue efforts will also face fear, despair, guilt and self-righteousness. I fear my friends and family will reject me once they know of my new relationship with Jesus. I fear the mockery and the confrontation of non-believers. I despair over the fate of loved ones who have rejected Christ and the secular trends that seem to be growing daily in enmity toward God. I feel guilty that I continue to fall short, despite knowing the urgency of the rescue mission and the price of failure. I look with self-righteousness on those who have not seen the clarity of Christ's love as I have. And running throughout all these perverse thoughts is the realization that unless I can come to grips with this culture shock, unless I can claim the mindset of survivor, then I will have debased the value of my own rescue…

Every successful survival story ends with rescue. We all have a survival story to tell. How will it end? When will we step out of danger and despair and into the arms of rescue? We cannot say. Indeed, we are not privy to the when, or the where, or the how (Matthew 24:36). But we do know the Who, and we do know the why.

We are not of this world, nor are we destined to remain here. Visit a nearby cemetery if you are in denial of this fact. Yet, while we remain, a comforter is ever present at our side. He has been assigned as our rescuer, and He is very, very good at what He does. He has never deserted those entrusted to Him, and He never will. He has never failed to save those who have cried out to Him, and He never will. Those who doubt this need only meditate upon His name and rank:

> Jesus: [Hebrew: "God with us"]. Is there anyone
> else you would rather have with you in a sur-
> vival situation than God Himself?

Christ: [Greek for Messiah: "One who saves."].
Is there any title more fitting for our personal
rescuer?

The "Why" is equally simple: Because He loves us.
Don't try to muddy this fact with talk of worthiness
or indebtedness or understanding or good deeds. Just
revel in its simplicity and live like one who appreciates
the fact.

Being a survivor, rescued through Jesus, is an intimately personal event, one that will bond you to God
in an incomprehensible way. You have been adopted
into a royal household (1Peter 2:19). Your life has been
purchased with blood (Ephesians 1:7). Your very name
is written in the palm of God's hand (Isaiah 49:16).
Rejoice! You are a survivor! Take comfort in this immu-
table fact, and enjoy the refreshment and renewal that
comes with being a member of the wedding feast. But
don't for a moment think that the mission has come to
an end.

Search Scripture for a passage that declares: The
best way to get through life is to go it alone. Or how
about: The man who strives to be a rugged individual
is a man to be admired. Or even: When the going gets
rough, hole up by yourself and prepare to make a stand.
You won't find such sentiments.

On the contrary, Scripture gives us passages like: It
is not good for the man to be alone (Genesis 2:18); A
cord of three strands is not easily broken (Ecclesiastes
4:12); two are better than one, because they have a good
return for their labor (Ecclesiastes 4:9). It is clear that
Christ invites us, even commands us, to go out in pairs,

to gather in groups of two or three, to come together as community, as church. And not just to gather, but to go forth and seek those who are lost, to reach out with the Good News and extend a message of hope and salvation. In short, once we are rescued we are called to be members of the rescue squad. The time is short. The task is great. The alarm bell is ringing, the SOS has gone out. How will we respond?

1. Having accepted Jesus as our rescuer, knowing how much He loves us, why does fear still inhabit our lives?
2. Prisoners sometimes fear liberty, soldiers sometimes dread peace, addicts fear leaving rehab. Why is this? Why do people fear committing themselves to Christ?
3. We ought to feel grief when we see the state of the world, especially the state of those closest to us. How do we prevent this grief from becoming despair?
4. Guilt stems from, "I should have…I shouldn't have…" Think of a loved one currently in crisis, and complete the following: "I will…I will not…"
5. There are those who follow the philosophy: You can't change the past; I have no regrets. Is this a Christian attitude?
6. Sometimes those saved by Christ come across as being pompous and condemning. What is a safety measure that can be used to prevent this attitude from getting in the way of the rescue mission?

7. What is the difference between being righteous and self-righteous?
8. What does it mean to have the mindset of a survivor? A rescuer?
9. Is there a place for the "lone" rescuer or must we all be part of a rescue team?
10. How will you respond to the fact that alarm klaxons are going off? Be specific.

BIBLIOGRAPHY

For medical descriptions of what happens to the human body under extreme conditions, I highly recommend Kenneth Kamler's Surviving the Extremes. For the psychological factors of survival, I have read none better than Laurence Gonzales' Deep Survival. The principles pertaining to first aid are those I learned while teaching for the American Red Cross; however, it should be noted that this manual is in no way a first-aid course, nor does it have any affiliation with the ARC. For practical wilderness survival skills, John Wiseman's classic, Survive Safely Anywhere is hard to beat. I am indebted to the United States Air Force Search and Rescue Survival Training manual for its insight on the mission and mindset of a downed pilot. For clarity of explanation, simplicity and downright usefulness, I would highly recommend Les Stroud's Survive! and Paul Tawrell's Camping and Wilderness Survival.

Gonzales, Laurence. *Deep Survival. Who Lives, Who Dies, and Why.* New York: W.W. Norton and Company, 2004.

Kamler, Kenneth. *Surviving the Extremes. What happens to the Body and Mind at the Limits of Human Endurance.* New York: Penguin Books, 2005.

Stroud, Les. *Survive! Essential Skills and Tactics to get you out of Anywhere-Alive.* New York: HarperCollins, 2008.

Tawrell, Paul. *Camping and Wilderness Survival.* Ontario, Canada: Tawrell, 1996.

Wiseman, John. *Survive Safely Anywhere. The SAS Survival Manual.* New York: Crown Publishers, Inc., 1986.

AF Regulation 64-4. *Search and Rescue Survival Training.* Washington, DC, 1985.